DESPERATE LANDS

THE WAR ON TERROR THROUGH THE EYES OF A SPECIAL FORCES SOLDIER

REGULO ZAPATA, JR.

Published by Nadores Publishing & Research
P.O. Box 1202
Gilroy, CA 95021-1202, USA
www.nadorespublishing.com

Printed in the United States of America

Editing and design by Page One Communications

While the author has made every effort to provide accurate
telephone numbers and Internet addresses at the time of
publication, neither the publisher nor the author assumes any
responsibility for errors or for changes that occur after publication.
Further, the publisher does not have any control over and does not
assume any responsibility for author or third-party websites or
their contents.

The names and identifying information of certain people depicted
in this book have been changed to protect their privacy
and for their security.

Photos and map sketches in this book are courtesy of the author.

First Edition, Third Printing

Library of Congress Control Number: 2007904879

ISBN-13: 978-0-9797847-0-5
ISBN-10: 0-9797847-0-0

CONTENTS

DEDICATION

Our prayers go to the soldiers who have given the ultimate sacrifice—and for those who came back injured from the global war on terrorism in Afghanistan and Iraq.

To all the families and parents who have sons and daughters still fighting in the war on terrorism.

To my wife and family, who sacrificed greatly as I served in the U.S.Army for twenty-eight years.

To my mother, Maria Teresa, who kept me in her prayers while I was in Afghanistan.

To all our forgotten friends—names and faces from the past— whose lives touched mine as I served in the military.

To my grandson, Caden Filice, who fought a battle of his own at five months of age.

ACKNOWLEDGMENTS

This book would not have been possible without the extraordinary support of a number of people.

I begin with my wife, Delia Zapata. Being married to a soldier in the U.S. Army Special Forces demands a lot of sacrifice and devotion from a military wife. Delia provided emotional support during the writing process and helped me arrive at the ideas reflected in the book.

I want to express my gratitude to my gifted editor, Ken McFarland—an author, editor, newspaper and magazine writer, television scriptwriter, and designer—for his careful effort in bringing this book to completion. During each stage of the editorial process as well as page layout and design, he has been insightful, meticulous, and enthusiastic. In sum, he has been an ideal editor and a valued friend.

I want to express my gratitude to Bobbie Christensen—a freelance writer, teacher, and publisher—for her mentorship and guidance in helping me develop a step-by-step approach to successfully writing, publishing, and marketing my book. She has been an inspirational friend.

I thank several good friends—John Brookins, Jim Willis, Hans Halberstadt, and Bill Lamos—who took time to read the manuscript and provide me with invaluable suggestions.

I thank each and every one, including those who remain unnamed, and their families, for their forbearance and their service to our country.

I want to express my gratitude to Sergeant Major Palacios, with 2nd Bn, 75th Rangers; Sergeant Major Rodolfo Teodosio, with 1st Special Forces Group; Master Sergeant John Allen with 2nd Bn, 75th Rangers; and Sergeant Major Matoon with 2nd Bn, 75th Rangers; for their mentorship and guidance in my becoming a U.S Army Special Forces noncommissioned officer.

PREFACE

It has been four years since I returned from the war in Afghanistan, yet the memories seem just as clear as if it were yesterday that I was there with my Operational Detachment Alpha 995 (ODA-995) on combat patrols.

It has taken me this long to work up the courage to decide to write this unbelievable story—my recollection of an extraordinary journey to hostile, desperate lands—to countries with strange ways of living as if still in ancient times.

While assigned to the Army National Guard, 19th Special Forces Group Airborne, I had the privilege of serving alongside the proud men and women in our nation's global war on terrorism.

My story begins with my telling you a little about myself. I first served several years in the U.S. Army, active duty, with the 2nd Battalion, 75th Rangers Airborne, at Fort Lewis, Washington. Thereafter, I was assigned to Bravo Company, 3rd Battalion, 5th Special Forces Group, Airborne, in Fort Bragg, North Carolina.

I graduated from the famous United States Army John F. Kennedy Special Warfare Center School, the Army Special Forces Operations and Intelligence Course, the United States Army Ranger School, and many other advanced Special Forces schools available to a Green Beret noncommissioned officer while on active duty.

I later transferred to join the U.S. Army Reserves 12th Special

Forces Group and, later still, transitioned into the California Army National Guard, 19th Special Forces Group Airborne. By this time, I had twenty-seven years serving in Special Operations Forces within the Department of the Army.

All my training and experience as a Special Forces soldier was now going to be put to work on the fight against global war on terrorism.

My full-time civilian occupation was working as a park ranger for the County of Santa Clara Parks & Recreation Agency in the state of California. To this day, I will never forget when my wife woke me up on September 11, 2001, to see the horrifying World Trade Center disaster in New York City on television. From that day on, everyone's lives changed. For the next five years and to this day, we are still at war because of the terrorist attacks on the United States.

"Honey wake up," my wife had said, "look at this on television. Something terrible is happening in New York City."

As I watched the events taking place at the World Trade Center, I was shocked to see the terror unfolding. My eyes did not believe what was happening. Was this a dream or a movie?

At the time of this awful event, I worked as the unit's operations sergeant with Alpha Company, 5th Battalion 19th Special Forces Group (Airborne). A few hours after the terrorists attacks on the World Trade Center, my unit urgently telephoned my home to tell me of the terrorist attacks in New York City and Washington, D.C. My unit officially placed everyone on standby alert, pending additional instructions on activation orders for our unit's deployment somewhere overseas.

A few months later, we found ourselves in strange, hostile, and desperate lands hunting and destroying the terrorist networks in the Horn of Africa and into the frontier borders of Pakistan and Afghanistan. The U.S. Army 3rd Special Forces Group was sent home as heroes, and we eagerly took their places, though ill equipped.

Many stories are told by retired generals and reporters who keep notebooks and journals. But I was a Special Forces enlisted soldier in the battlefield. I hope these stories will convey some of the reality of the times and places involved. I have many stories to tell, and if a few of them get read, maybe someone will learn what happened with those of us fighting the secret, front-line war on terrorism in Africa and Afghanistan.

My stories will not alleviate the suffering of many families who have sons and daughters fighting in the war on terrorism. But they may help my readers understand what it was really like for a Special Forces team and its team sergeant.

I now sit at home with my wife and worry about our only son, who is now in Iraq for a second tour, serving as an infantry soldier with the United States Army 4th Infantry Division.

WHAT READERS ARE SAYING

"An exciting read and fascinating journey. A must-read this year."
—Chief Warrant Officer John Brookins, U.S. Army Special Forces, 19th Special Forces Group Airborne.

"Excellent read! Regulo gives a detailed, emotional description of the efforts of Special Forces to hunt down terrorists in Africa and in Afghanistan and bring them to justice."
—Major Bill Lamos, United States Air Force (Retired).

"Master Sgt. Regulo Zapata has written a fascinating account of life inside a contemporary Special Forces Operational Detachment ALPHA as it conducts missions around the world. Zapata is a member of the 'old breed' of SF sergeants and provides a career professional's perspective on this small community of warrior-brothers that couldn't be written by anybody but a 'Green Beret.' This book describes how an ODA works as it gears up for battle and then executes its many missions in strange places around the globe. A good addition to the bookshelf of anyone interested in special operations forces at war."
—Hans Halberstadt, author, *Roughneck Nine-One* and *War Stories of the Green Berets.*

INTRODUCTION

This is the story of Army Special Forces soldiers and the missions they carried out in fighting the global war on terrorism in the Horn of Africa and in Afghanistan. This book seeks to convey the reality of Army Special Forces efforts, by recounting missions carried out by soldiers during their year-long tour with the Army National Guard 19th Special Forces Group, Airborne.

The stories are told through the eyes of one senior noncommissioned officer known as the team sergeant of Operational Detachment Alpha 995 (ODA-995).

The names and identifying information of certain people depicted in this book have been changed to protect their privacy.

The goal is to give the reader a realistic view of Special Forces soldiers going through their everyday operations while in the Horn of Africa and later on in Afghanistan.

These pages will share the sacrifice, bravery, horror, fear, and life of U.S. Army Special Forces soldiers in the Horn of Africa and in Afghanistan. It tells the story of our nation's struggle and of the soldiers fighting a new and different kind of war—a kind of war never fought before: the global war on terror. This war continues at a time when our nation has mixed and divided feelings—both among our government leaders and the American people—concerning this new war on terrorism.

The first three chapters to follow will recount missions leading into the Horn of Africa by Master Sergeant Zapata during his first surveillance operations on terrorist networks.

Chapter 4 describes ODA-995, 5th Battalion, 19th Special Forces Group mobilization—and their mandatory Special Forces certification and qualification at Fort Carson, Colorado, prior to entering the war in Afghanistan.

Chapters 5 through 15 will narrate ODA-995's numerous missions in Afghanistan. Chapter 16 will give an account of Army Special Forces Group personnel returning from the war in Afghanistan and provide an update on what has happened to these soldiers now.

To this day, the secret war on global terrorism continues behind the scenes, fought bravely by U.S. Army Special Forces soldiers.

In December 2006 and January 2007, U.S. Special Operation Forces located terrorist operatives in Somalia and conducted U.S. air strikes there on terrorist targets. No one can know what comes next, except that for as long as free people cherish their freedom, its defense will continue.

CHAPTER ONE

REPORTING FOR DUTY

Several weeks after the terrorist attacks in New York City and in Washington D.C., a U.S. military unit called Special Operations Command Central (SOCCENT) was busy planning missions and recruiting personnel with certain military occupational skills.

SOCCENT had sent the recruiting request to all Special Forces Army National Guard battalions. Also, SOCCENT was recruiting Army Special Forces operations and intelligence sergeants for specific missions to support operations of the Global War on Terror.

My name came up on my unit's manning roster, listed as a qualified special operations and intelligence sergeant. Within a few days I received my orders from SOCCENT to report for duty.

SOCCENT exercises command and control of all elite United States and foreign joint special operations task forces deployed in Afghanistan. My orders were to report to SOCCENT at MacDill Air Force Base, Florida. The orders stated that the duration of my duty time was six months and that my move to MacDill was considered a Permanent Change of Station (PCS). I was allowed four days of travel time by vehicle to reach MacDill in Florida.

As is far too typical, my military orders were all fucked up and had some major errors. I was not able to get paid per diem travel, family separation allowance, basic allowance for housing, or hostile fire and imminent pay. It was a total nightmare.

It ultimately took four months to correct the errors on the military orders and finally to be paid. It took weeks just to amend the military orders. Meanwhile, my bills at home were not being paid. My understanding of the payroll problem was that a glitch in the payroll system between the Army National Guard Bureau and the Department of the Army Finance was an ongoing fiasco resulting in delayed payment to Army National Guard soldiers. I was not the only ANG solider with pay problems. The horror stories I heard from some of the other soldiers were unbelievable.

As I began traveling from my hometown of Gilroy, California, by vehicle, I was able to enjoy some of the scenic desert Southwest views while traveling thru Arizona and New Mexico. Finally, I arrived in San Antonio, Texas, to visit my parents. But I was able to rest for only a few hours at my parents' home before continuing on to MacDill Air Force Base, Florida.

All I remember before leaving the next morning was watching my nervous mother preparing a nice breakfast for me. I saw the concern on my poor mother's face—and listened to a mother's prayers and the blessings she gave me before I left on my journey.

Luckily, I arrived one day early at MacDill. I was able there to talk to an old friend who had earlier been an enlisted U.S. Army Special Forces sergeant and was now a Special Forces officer. Captain Carmona lived in Tampa, Florida, with his wife and two kids. He had recently returned from Afghanistan and shared some of his horrifying stories with me. I'll always remember his wife's hospitality in preparing for us every day a huge feast of a breakfast and dinner while I stayed in their home. I was able to stay there for a few days until I was deployed elsewhere with SOCCENT. My orders were to work in the SOCCENT Joint J-3 Operations Center doing I wasn't sure what yet, until I was filled in later on.

On my first day I arrived at 7 a.m. at Special Operations Command Central for in-processing. I was met by an Army officer named Captain Omar who worked in the SOCCENT's Special Projects, Joint J-3 Operations area.

Captain Omar was a 7th Special Forces Group soldier—a combat veteran. His facial appearance suggested a Middle Eastern or Arabic ethnic background. Captain Omar escorted me into the building to meet a Major Johnson, who was in charge of the Joint J-3 Operations Center.

As I walked into the room, Captain Omar introduced Major Johnson.

"Major Johnson, this is Master Sergeant Zapata from 19th Special Forces Group, California. He has arrived to this unit and is assigned to your section."

I looked at Major Johnson and saw a smile on his face—and both another officer and another sergeant sitting in the back room, staring at me.

"Sergeant Zapata, welcome to SOCCENT. I have been waiting for you. I hope you had a good flight here, Sarge?"

Major Johnson was a tall, slim-looking combat veteran wearing a desert uniform and sizeably muscular for a desk officer.

"Sergeant Zapata, I want to introduce our staff in J-3 Operations. This is Major Sims, United States Marine Corps, our Operations Officer—and Sergeant First Class Thomas, an Army Special Forces Operations Sergeant."

Major Sims was a tall, slim Force Recon Marine Officer, with a desert uniform and a short military haircut. Sergeant First Class Thomas was a short, medium-built, thin-looking man from 5th Special Forces Group—a combat veteran also, dressed in his desert uniform.

All three men had recently returned from the "Box"—a military term meaning the battlefield in Afghanistan. They were now assigned to SOCCENT in support of Operation Enduring Freedom.

"Master Sergeant Zapata, I want you to continue your in-process as soon as possible. Once you have done this, we will give you a complete intelligence briefing on what our ground forces are doing in Afghanistan in connection with the Global War on Terrorism."

SOCCENT had given me an in-process checklist to follow. It took about two days to complete the in-processing to bring me into the unit. By this time, I had my medical records, power of attorney, and soldier group life insurance (SGLI) checked, and complete battle gear equipment was issued to me.

I was led to believe, that I was going to serve my six months in support of Operation Enduring Freedom at SOCCENT here at MacDill. I imagined how great this duty was going to be. I had nice weather was already enjoying beautiful, sandy white ocean beaches. I was planning to have my wife fly to Tampa for vacations and visits.

Shit!

I was in for a rude awakening once I reported back to Major Johnson, the Joint J-3 Operations commander.

"Master Sergeant Zapata, please take a seat. We will brief you on the situation in Afghanistan and the Global War on Terror and explain what your duty position will be and where you are going."

I immediately asked myself, "Going where? And doing what?" Major Johnson, SFC Thomas, and Major Sims continued to give me their intelligence briefing on the war situation in Afghanistan and in other parts of the world. By the time I departed the room, I had a good idea as to what our Special Operations forces and regular ground forces were trying to accomplish in Afghanistan and in the Global War on Terror.

My orders now were to depart from SOCCENT within the next eight hours with other Special Operations personnel to a country called Doha, Qatar. I was to serve at the Joint Operations Center as the noncommissioned officer in charge of Combined Joint Forces Special Operations Component Command, Special Operations Command Central, at Camp As Sayliyah, Qatar.

Wow! What in the fuck had these people gotten me involved in? Within a few hours following my briefing I was packing all my personal equipment to meet other Special Operations personnel by 5 a.m. The next day my friend Captain Carmona transported me to the MacDill Air Force Base terminal and began loading the aircraft.

Within moments I was flying to Doha, Qatar.

CHAPTER TWO

QATAR JOINT OPERATIONS CENTER

We had been flying for over six hours when the Air Force pilots announced that we were preparing to arrive in the country of Bahrain for refueling. We spent two hours there refueling the aircraft, in extremely hot weather conditions.

As we unloaded some items from the aircraft, I recall seeing several fully armed security force Marines surrounding the aircraft and the terminal taxi area we were on. Once the aircraft was refueled we were on our way again to Doha, Qatar. After a few more hours, the pilots announced that we were arriving in Doha.

I looked at my watch and noted it was 3 a.m. Once on the ground in Qatar, we began to unload the Air Force C-17 transport aircraft. I could feel the immediate blast of heat and humidity as I stepped outside the aircraft. It felt as if the aircraft's own engines were blowing hot air against my face.

As I walked a distance away from the aircraft, I noticed that it was pitch dark out—and no lights were being used. I was unable even to see the person in front of me. All I remember was hearing the voice of a black female Air Force sergeant giving orders directing us to load onto a bus to be transported to our next location.

The drive to Camp As Sayliyah took approximately an hour. As we arrived there, an Army first sergeant began instructing us on what tents we would occupy for the duration of the mission. The first sergeant also gave us the time and location for reporting to the Joint Operations Center for a briefing in the morning.

It was already 4 a.m., and I was feeling tired. I still had two hours before time to report for the briefing, so I decided to get some sleep. Almost before I knew it, my watch alarm started ringing, and it was time to get up. It felt as if I had only slept for a few seconds! I quickly looked at my watch, and it was already 6 a.m.

I opened the tent flaps, and a bright orange-red sun glared into my eyes, momentarily blinding me. The heat of the day already felt as if it were coming from a large, open oven. I was sweating like a pig as I began walking away from the tent.

Looking around, I saw nothing but yellow sand—no trees, no plants, no birds. The heat was unbearable. I could see several shelter-bunker positions made of sandbags, military tents, large metal warehouses, military vehicles, and military personnel moving about like busy ants.

I looked at my watch and saw I had twenty minutes to get to the Joint Operations Center for the briefing. As I reached the main entrance, I had to go thru a security checkpoint to gain access to the building. Waiting outside, I saw a temperature gauge on the wall near the entrance. I looked at it several times and finally spoke to the soldier near the entrance.

"Hey, sergeant, is that temperature gauge reading correctly?"

The temp showed as 133 degrees!

"Yeah, it's correct—and working," the soldier replied with a smile. "I must be in hell—or at least near hell," I returned.

Moments later, a Captain Lee arrived at the entrance to escort me into the building to meet the Joint Operations commander. Captain Lee was a tall, slim Asian-looking U.S. Army Ranger from the Ranger Regiment, working as battle captain in the JOC. Once inside the Center, I saw several officers with laptop computers, busy typing, reading, or preparing for the staff briefing beginning in a few minutes to be given to the Joint Operations commander and other generals.

I had arrived in time to sit in on and listen to a full situation briefing on the status of enemy forces, coalition ground forces, and American forces in Afghanistan and other regions in the world. Once the briefing was finished, Captain Lee introduced the Joint Operations commander and sergeant major to me. My whole day was spent talking to them, getting oriented to the JOC, familiarizing myself with my duties and responsibilities, and meeting the JOC staff.

I had noticed that the Joint Operations Center was staffed by American Army, Marine, Navy, and Air Force officers. The sergeant major and I were the only two enlisted personnel working inside the JOC.

Later in the evening I stepped outside the JOC building to take a rest and watch an enormous sun setting, Suddenly, I began to hear a loud Islamic call to prayer—Muslims chanting one of their five daily prayers. The *muezzin*—a crier who calls the faithful to prayer—chanted aloud from a high tower in the mosque near our firebase.

I found myself listening to this eerie sound and wondering who this chanting person was and what was he saying as he chanted aloud to all of us. As I listened, I felt as if I were in some faraway evil, strange, remote, desert land in some French Foreign Legion outpost, waiting for an attack by hundreds of Muslims.

This same prayer chant was heard everyday throughout Africa and Afghanistan. I found the call to prayer chant to be tense and unique. This was my first experience in listening to this Muslism world culture—in a call to prayer chant.

Two months had passed working as the Joint Operations sergeant, and I was already getting to know almost all the officers in the unit. It was interesting to see that almost all of them were either Reserve or Army National Guard personnel I later learned that two of the officers, by the names of Major Stanley and Major Pound, were officers from the same 5th Battalion, 19th Special Forces Group to which I belonged. Little did I know that I would later be working together closely with both of these excellent officers in future operations in Afghanistan.

Major Stanley was a tall, slim officer with short, brown hair and was responsible for giving daily situational briefing updates on the training of the Afghanistan National Army ground forces and the operations they were executing.

Major Pound was also tall—a muscular man with medium-to-short, dark-black hair. He was responsible for giving daily situational briefings on the European Joint Coalition Ground Forces in Afghanistan and the operations they were executing. Both officers had just recently returned from several missions in Afghanistan and were now assigned to work in support of Operation Enduring Freedom while in Qatar at the JOC.

The center operated twenty-four hours a day, seven days a week. All personnel worked fourteen hours a day or more—and for us, it was getting tedious. In the early mornings when it was cooler, I found myself running laps around the firebase and lifting weights just to stay in good physical condition—and to relieve stress from my work.

As I was working one afternoon, I received a message from the U.S. Air Force Special Operations Command, in desperate need of one Special Forces, force protection level-II serviceman. The Air Force wanted someone to conduct a high-threat vulnerability assessment on a Special Forces advanced operational base with a landing zone in Djibouti, Africa.

The situation was this: The United States had staged special operations forces at a remote firebase called Camp Lemonier, in Djibouti. The Advanced Operational Base (AOB) would conduct clandestine operations and disrupt Taliban and Al Qaeda networks operating in the surrounding region of the Horn of Africa.

In order for the Air Force to support and execute these types of operations in the region, it would require the Air Force to have aircraft permanently stationed in Djibouti, with sufficient firepower and transportation capabilities for special operations personnel.

Due to the high level of terrorist threat in the region—and because of insufficient force protection level and lack of security personnel to safeguard aircraft and personnel in Camp Lemonier—the Air Force would not station fixed-wing aircraft in Djibouti unless a Force Protection Level Plan was prepared and given to the Air Force Special Operations Command.

The U.S. Air Force wanted a guarantee of security force protection of all its aircraft permanently parked in Djibouti. Therefore, the Joint Operations Center in Qatar had to send a qualified person to Djibouti, to conduct a threat vulnerability assessment of the firebase, landing zone, personnel security, and Djibouti harbors and waterways.

This is where I came into the picture, being the only qualified Special Operations, force protection level sergeant working in the Joint Operations Center in Qatar. Because of the urgency of the situation in Djibouti, I was chosen for this assignment.

Someone had earlier told me, "Never volunteer for something when you do not know what you're getting involved in."

I believed I had just broken the first rule in war: never volunteer for anything in a combat zone!

Four hours later, I was flying to Djibouti, Africa.

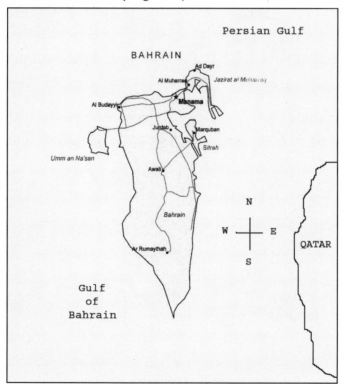

Bahrain aircraft refueling location

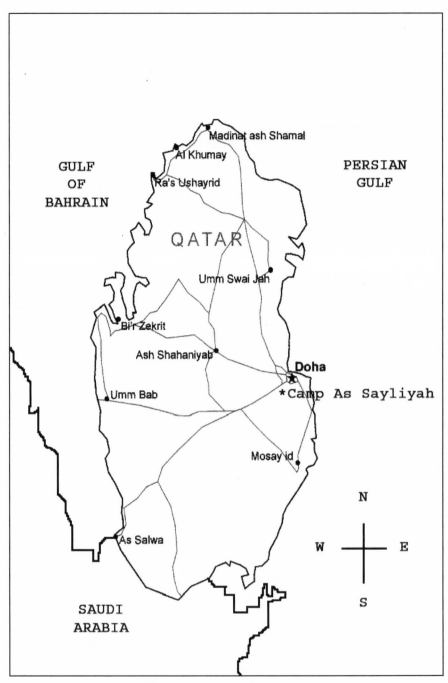

Camp As Sayliyah, Qatar

CHAPTER THREE

CAMP LEMONIER FIREBASE— DJIBOUTI, AFRICA

Within four hours I was flying into Djibouti, Africa, to conduct my Threat Vulnerability Assessment mission.

Another USMC officer named Major Allen was flying to Djibouti with me. Major Allen was a Special Operations Marine, tasked by Special Operations Command Central (SOCCENT) to troubleshoot in resolving an officer power dispute between two commanders: a U.S. Army colonel serving as firebase commander—and a U.S. Air Force colonel.

Neither officer would cooperate with the other, because of a dispute as to who was the overall firebase commander in charge while in Djibouti. This was creating friction between Army, Air Force, and Navy Special Operations Forces in executing their missions.

Another issue was that a platoon-sized Marine fleet anti-terrorist security team—providing temporary security for the firebase in Djibouti—was being ordered to redeploy elsewhere within a few days.

As we were in flight to Djibouti, the aircraft was redirected by SOCCENT to land at the Sur Masirah, Oman firebase. Sur Masirah is an island located off the coast of Oman on the Arabian Sea. The SOCCENT there spoke to us over the radio and ordered us to link up with one company of a Marine Expeditionary Task Force and with Special Operations forces located in Sur Masirah island.

A U.S. Navy Carrier Air Group was positioned several miles off the Arabian Sea coast of Oman in support of this operation, providing air support and air transportation for the troops.

A top Al-Qaeda terrorist network group leader—and other members who had played a key role in attacks against U.S. embassies in Africa—had been located near Habrut, Yemen, by Joint U.S. Special Operations Forces conducting live surveillance on the target.

The immediate plan was to send one company of Marines to provide support and security for the target, while Joint U.S. Special Forces assault elements would attack the target and capture the Al Qaeda leader and other members.

When we arrived at the Sur Masirah firebase, Major Allen began coordinating with Marine Task Force commanders. I watched as Marines and Joint Special Operations personnel rested on the tarmac of the airstrip in full combat battle gear, waiting to load approaching Navy Ch-46 helicopters coming from a Navy carrier air group.

The soldiers were adjusting their rucksacks, packing equipment, distributing live ammunition—hand grenades—and inspecting their weapons.

I continued watching as four Ch-46 helicopters began to land, while Marines and Special Operations personnel quickly stood up and moved toward the helicopters to load. Moments later, I began to hear the loud engines and the even louder sound of the rotary blades turning, as the helicopters lifted off the ground and headed toward the horizon.

Marines and Army Special Operations personnel loading Ch-46 helicopters—this would be one mission I would not be participating in. But later on I would read a Mission Concept Letter (MICON), once back at Joint Operations Center in Qatar.

I was astonished to see the living conditions at the U.S. Air Force firebase in Sur Masirah, compared to U.S. Army firebases. At night the firebase, with all its brightly colored lights, reminded me of a night in the city of New Orleans during the Mardi Gras parade.

Several tents had Christmas lights hanging outside. The firebase had an excellent mess hall, where you could eat steaks, lobster, and ice cream. They had an area where you could drink cold beers, enjoy eating popcorn, and watch a movie inside a building with air conditioning. The weather conditions and temperature was extremely hot and unbearable due to the dry desert, no winds and hot sun in Sur Masirah island.

A large number of U.S. Air Force females worked inside the firebase. Wow! The U.S. Air Force definitely knew how to care for the health and welfare of their soldiers, compared to the U.S. Army. The following morning, Major Allen and I flew out from the island of Sur Masirah, Oman on a C-17 transport aircraft and arrived in Camp Lemonier. As the rear ramp door opened, I felt the extreme heat blowing on my face, and as I began to walk down the ramp, I heard the loud jet engines roaring. The C-17 kept its engines running, as it was doing a quick, hot unloading of personnel and supplies for the Advance Operational Base.

Members of the Army 3rd Special Forces Group were waiting for us at the Camp Lemonier airstrip to transport us to the firebase commander. As we approached the inner security perimeter of the firebase, I saw several sandbag bunkers, twenty-foot-tall metal fences, and observation towers along the perimeter, which was also guarded by armed soldiers.

I saw five wooden buildings and seven large GP tents in the center of the firebase. I also saw two U.S. Air Force MH-53 helicopters, well armed with 50-caliber machine guns on the rear ramp doors and 7.62-mm mini-guns on each of the side doors of the aircraft.

U.S. Joint Special Forces personnel in Camp Lemonier included one U.S. Army Special Forces group team, one U.S. Navy Seal team, one U.S. Air Force Para-Rescue Team, one U.S. Marine platoon from the Fleet Antiterrorist Security Team (FAST), and one Army Service Support section—all totaled, about eighty-three personnel on the Camp Lemonier firebase.

As Major Allen and I walked into the commander's office, Army Lieutenant Colonel Jones introduced himself.

"Major Allen and Sergeant Zapata, welcome to Camp Lemonier. I have been waiting for both of you. I hope you had an enjoyable flight here. Sergeant Zapata, I understand you are the force protection NCO assigned to the firebase. Please begin your threat vulnerability assessment of Camp Lemonier as soon as possible.

"Link up with Captain Smith from the United States Marine Corps Fleet Anti-Terrorist Security Team, who is providing security for the firebase. Have him show you around so you can understand what problems we are facing here at Camp Lemonier as far as force protection goes. You also need to meet with Air Force Lieutenant Colonel Bailey, in charge of the 20th Special Operations Squadron here on the firebase. He will be able to give you his concerns on aircraft force protection.

"We also have an Army Special Forces detachment and a Navy Seal team assigned to the firebase. I want you to meet as soon as possible with both of the team commanders. Please brief me on the status of the force protection plans during our next 4:00 p.m. staff meetings."

"Yes, Sir," I replied. "I will give you an update on the firebase force protection preparations as soon as I have something."

I walked out from the commander's office, leaving Major Allen with LTC Jones for their private meeting. I knew they were going to talk about officer business issues and mission tasking.

I located the building where Marine Captain Smith was located. As I walked into the building, I saw several other Marines in a small office room—the Tactical Operations Center (TOC) for the Marine Fleet Anti-Terrorism Security Team. As I entered, a Marine Captain said, "How can I help you, Top?"

"Yes, Sir—my name is Master Sergeant Zapata, Army Special Forces, assigned as the force protection sergeant at this firebase. I am looking for a Captain Smith."

"Sergeant Zapata, I am Captain Smith. I have been waiting for you. I am glad you are here. Take a seat, sergeant. Let me give you a quick situation update."

By the end of the day Captain Smith had given me a complete tour of the firebase and had shared his concerns about the need for additional security personnel and equipment to continue security on the firebase.

Later that evening, I met with both the Army 3rd Special Forces team commander and Navy Seal team commander. Both teams had been focusing on their own mission tasking. There is not too much that I am able to say about both Special Forces teams, as they both operated in secret for their missions.

Although, as the firebase force protection sergeant, I needed to familiarize myself with their concerns within the firebase and the surrounding area, I later learned that both Special Forces teams had established two separate, unknown, secret firebases in Djibouti. These two secret firebases were occupied, at least, by half teams, while the other half of the team was being staged here at the Advanced Operational Base—Camp Lemonier. Locations of these firebases were unknown.

During my meeting with the Army Special Forces team commander, I met an old Army Reserve 12th Special Forces Group friend by the name of Sergeant First Class Ferra, assigned to the Army 3rd Special Forces team as the operations and intelligence sergeant. Thanks to Sergeant First Class Ferras's information on enemy situation in the region, I was able better to prepare the Force Protection Plan in Djibouti.

One week had passed in my work as the force protection sergeant, and the Threat Vulnerability Assessment Plan needed more development. The force protection work was enormous, and I had requested two more force protection personnel to assist with the force protection plan and personnel training.

I sent a message to Special Operations Command Central, Camp As Sayliyah, Qatar. I requested additional security and engineering personnel for the firebase. We needed additional security personnel to secure the airfields near the firebase, and needed heavy equipment to build deep trenches and high dirt berms around the firebase.

Special Operations Command Central replied that I would have additional personnel and engineering construction equipment within seven days. Sixty infantry personnel from the West Virginia

DESPERATE LANDS

Army National Guard unit would be arriving, and four Army Engineer personnel would be arriving also.

To this day, I will never forget when the Virginia Army National Guard arrived on a C-17 aircraft at 3 a.m. in Camp Lemonier. Marine commander Captain Smith and his Marines had secured the entire landing zone for the aircraft. As I watched it land and taxi toward my location, I could hear the loud jet engines as it drew nearer.

The Air Force was doing a "hot unloading" of personnel and equipment, so the aircraft engines would not be shutting down. Time was therefore of the essence. It was a clear, full-moon night, incredibly hot, and I felt the stuffy humidity in the air. I was sweating like a pig as I stood there watching while the rear ramp door of the aircraft opened. As it lowered, I could see the red lights and personnel inside.

The Virginia Army National Guard personnel were wearing their full combat battle gear as they started to unload. The soldiers began unloading rucksacks, ammunition boxes, meals ready to eat (MREs), and other equipment and containers.

We had four five-ton cargo trucks and three Hummers ready for loading up this new personnel and equipment. Instructions were given to Second Lieutenant Williams, commander of the National Guard unit, to load all personnel and equipment into the vehicles.

The National Guard contingent was transported inside the firebase and settled into the living quarters where they would spend the next several months. Once the unit had finished unpacking and storing their equipment, they moved out to occupy security positions around the firebase perimeter.

By 1 p.m. the faces of the National Guard soldiers showed exhaustion from the extreme heat. Before long three of the personnel fainted from heat exhaustion and dehydration. They had not yet acclimatized to the extreme hot weather in Djibouti.

The Marine Corps was happy to see that the Army National Guard was now taking over responsibility for security on the firebase. This meant that the Marines could leave Djibouti soon and join their Marine Corps security force battalion. In the days immediately following, I spent many hours establishing a priority of work schedules for base and airfield fortifications. I also provided localized training to replacement security force, in order to meet mission requirements such as vehicle search procedures, use of force, and emergency alert procedures on the firebase.

My second week at Camp Lemonier, I received an urgent message from Special Operations Command Central (SOCCENT) in Qatar. I was to meet with a Central Intelligence Agency officer, an Air Force Office of Special Investigation (AFOSI) counterintelligence agent, and an Office of Naval Intelligence (ONI) counterintelligence agent at the U.S. Djibouti embassy.

I was to meet with a Mr. Clark from the CIA and a Mr. Golden—a foreign service officer in the U.S. Embassy. The meeting was to discuss and conduct a joint Threat Vulnerability Assessment Plan for the following areas: the U.S. Djibouti embassy; the city of Djibouti; the Djibouti airport; and all waterways, channels, ports, and harbors.

The Djibouti ports and harbors were in a strategic position near the shipping lanes passing thru the Gulf of Aden into the Red Sea and passing through the Suez Canal. Activity was high on ships and narco-terrorism networks operating in the area. This region is known as the mouth of the Horn of Africa to many people in the world.

As I arrived at the U.S. embassy, I noticed that the security guard at the main entrance of the embassy was not an American security contractor or a U.S. Marine, but a local Djibouti security contactor. I don't even remember the name of the security company. As I approached the entrance gate, the security guard checked my identification card and gave me access to enter the embassy facility.

The front outer perimeter security walls and the embassy building itself were well built and fortified with concrete barricades. The perimeter had twenty-foot-high concrete walls and a high steel fence. As I walked into the building, I came into an open lobby with a desk, where an American employee asked, "How can I help you"

"Yes, Sir, my name is Sergeant Zapata, U.S. Army Special Forces, and I am looking for a Mr. Golden or Mr. Clark for a meeting today."

"The meeting is being held in Room 105," the employee replied, "down the hallway to the right."

As I walked into the conference room, I saw several personnel sitting around chatting with each other. I was able to get the attention of one man sitting at the head of the conference table.

"Afternoon, Sir—my name is Sergeant Zapata, U.S. Army Special Forces. I am here to meet a Mr. Clark or a Mr. Golden."

"Welcome, Sergeant Zapata, to the U.S. Djibouti Embassy. I am Mr. Golden, the foreign service officer for the embassy. Please take a seat, and let me introduce you to several people here in the room.

"First, this is Mr. Brown, the U.S. Djibouti Ambassador; Mr. Clark of the Central Intelligence Agency; Mr. Nelson from the Office of Naval Intelligence; Mr. Franco, Air Force Office of Special Investigation; and Mrs. Judith from the Other Group Organization."

Mr. Brown was a tall, thin Asian-American man who appeared to be in his late 40s. Mr. Clark was a tall, slim Caucasian-appearing man wearing reading glasses, who also appeared to be in his late 40s. Mr. Nelson was a tall African-American man with short hair and a muscular build. Mr. Franco was a man with long, dark hair and a medium build, who appeared to be of Italian or Spanish descent. Mr. Golden was a tall, thin built individual and appeared to be in his late 40s, with short dark hair and a mustache. He appeared to be of European descent because of his deep French or German accent as he spoke to me. Mrs. Judith was a very attractive, slim, Caucasian appearing lady with very long brown hair, who appeared to be in her late 30s. She appeared to be of Middle Eastern descent because of her accent in speaking to everyone.

In the next few hours, we discussed several concerns Mr. Clark had concerning threat vulnerability to the personnel working in the U.S. Embassy—and about terrorist networks operating in the area. We concluded that the embassy needed U.S. Marines to provide full-time security.

In the following days Mr. Franco, Mr. Nelson, and I continued target surveillances and site surveys, on the Djibouti airport; on harbors, ports, routes, and roads; the Iraq Embassy; hotels; and the Djibouti Market Bazaar areas. My first live surveillance was on an

Ethiopian commercial aircraft with Al-Qaeda personnel transporting and unloading weapons and tons of *khat* drugs from an Ethiopian aircraft.

Khat contains caffeine and ephedrine-like compounds. It grows in a large shrub which eventually grows to tree size. The Khat leaf is chewed by natives as a stimulant to dispel feelings of hunger and fatigue. Those using it could become as high as if using cocaine. This meant that if I were attacked by any of these people, I would need to fire several bullet rounds into any of these doped-up subjects in order to stop them from hurting me.

Mr. Franco and I moved into a surveillance site forty-eight hours prior to the Ethiopian aircraft's arrival. We selected a good hiding site that would conceal us while still providing good visibility. We had more than enough time to set up our surveillance equipment. We had both the AN/PRC-117 and MBITR radios for communications, surveillance cameras, binocs, and other equipment. Both of us were carrying M4/M4A1, 5.56mm rifles and M-9, 9mm Beretta pistols as weapons protection.

The days were long and extremely hot, and we were starting to get restless and tired. I kept asking myself what the hell I was doing out here and thinking that there wasn't any shit going to happen today.

Mr. Clark and Mr. Nelson monitored radio communications between both teams. They were in a mobile vehicle able to observe and follow Al-Qaeda movements to their safehouse and storage of the cargo.

Later, in the afternoon of our second day, I saw a large green aircraft approaching the landing zone. As the aircraft approached the runway, I felt my heart beating harder and grew more excited as I wondered what—or whom—we would be observing. We watched every move of the aircraft as it taxied. I could see a truck with a trailer attached and other vehicles approaching the aircraft.

Several armed personnel, carrying AK-47 rifles and one RPG-7 (rocket propelled grenade) weapon approached and encircled the aircraft. The side cargo door opened, and a large truck and trailer backed into the opened door and several armed personnel from inside the aircraft exited. The terrorist group worked like ants, loading large white bagged bundles of khat onto the truck and trailer. It must have taken thirty minutes for them to unload all the khat bundles, along with several boxes of ammunition and weapons, onto the truck and trailer.

As we observed the activity, we recorded everything. We tried to photograph and identify any new Al-Qaeda leadership and other members during this operation. We took photos of the aircraft, pilots, vehicles, drivers, and anybody in a leadership or authority position. The mission was successful. Mr. Clark and Mr. Nelson were able to follow the shipment and identify the location of the terrorist network safehouse and cache site.

This would be sufficient intelligence data for a follow-up mission package for U.S. Special Forces personnel, to prepare and execute a direct action strike on these targets later on.

Several weeks passed, and I executed several surveillance operations in the region. The firebase Threat Vulnerability Assessment Plan was completed, and I was ordered to return to Special Operations Command Central in Camp As Sayliyah, Qatar.

As I flew back to Qatar, I remembered the situation in Djibouti. I was amazed both by how exotic the country was and by how poor the living conditions were for the people who lived there. Djibouti was vulnerable to outsiders, as terrorist network groups found it easy to operate there and find refuge in an unsecured country. I also remembered the U.S. soldiers still working in miserable conditions and how secret this whole war of fighting and locating terrorist was.

Once in Qatar, I was welcomed back and thanked many times by the Camp As Sayliyah commander and sergeant major for a job well done. It was nice to be back in a much safer location and in better living conditions with excellent meals and cool showers.

I had been overseas about four months when I received a message from my unit commander that our entire 5th Battalion, 19th Special Forces Group was being activated and mobilized to deploy into Afghanistan within the next forty-five days. My orders were to return to my unit ASAP. My unit gave me one week's travel time to return back to my unit to conduct the unit's mobilization process, which was taking place at Camp Roberts, California Army National Guard Center.

Within three days I was flying out of Doha, Qatar, and arriving in SOCCENT MacDill Air Force Base, Florida. I was now to travel on a new journey into a faraway strange land which I knew nothing about. As I wondered about Afghanistan, I was not yet able to see light at the end of the tunnel. The rumor was that I would deploy for between six months and a year in Afghanistan.

Before I knew it, I was on my way back to my unit in California.

Marines and Army Special Operations personnel loading CH-46 helicopters.

Four MH-53 helicopter gunships

Rear entrance to Djibouti Firebase

Camp Lemonier main entrance

Army National Guard Infantry Security Force

Front main entrance to Djibouti Firebase

Army National Guard doing vehicle search

Surveillance on Al-Qaeda unloading Khat and weapons

Djibouti Ports & Harbors entrance

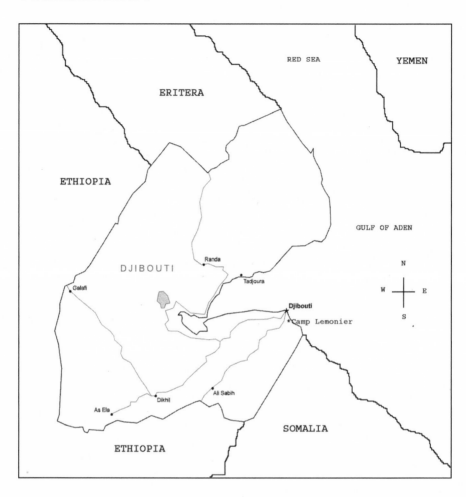

Djibouti, Africa, shipping lanes

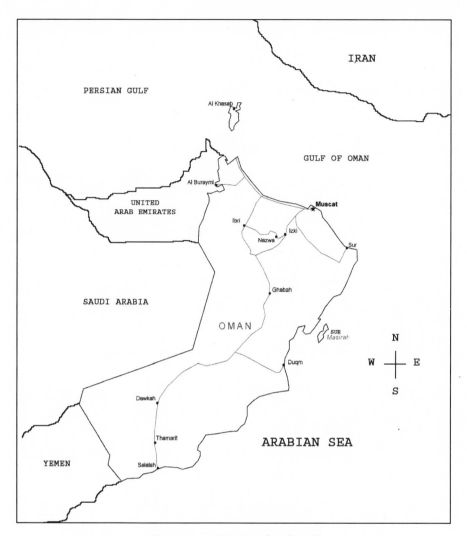

Oman — Masirah Island

CHAPTER FOUR

FORT CARSON, COLORADO, UNIT STAGING AREA

The entire 5th Battalion, 19th Special Forces Group was being sent to Fort Carson, Colorado. Our entire battalion occupied old World War II barracks at Fort Carson, Colorado, for the next four or five weeks.

Our first week was easy—doing physical training in the mornings and mobilization in-processing all day. We received a complete medical examination, had our vaccinations; reviewed Soldiers Group Life Insurance (SGLI), selected our power of attorney, and updated our personal security clearance.

Rumor had it that we would be spending thirty days going through Special Forces certification evaluation prior to leaving for Afghanistan. An announcement was given to all detachment commanders and team sergeants that only the teams scoring highest on their Special Forces certification and evaluation would have first pick of the missions their detachments would execute once in Afghanistan.

The Mission Tasking was to conduct Foreign Internal Defense (FID) in training the Afghanistan National Army, Strategic Reconnaissance (SR) on terrorist targets, and also Direct Action (DA) strike missions on terrorist targets. The idea was to create more competition between the detachments in fighting for their missions.

For some of the soldiers this seemed like a bunch of bullshit, but others liked the idea of the competition. Before the Special Forces certification and evaluation period, the company commander told me that I was going to be assigned and deploying with another company as the detachment operations sergeant. I was now being assigned to Operational Detachment Alpha 995, Charlie Company, 5th Battalion, 19th Special Forces Group Airborne, as the operations sergeant for the A-Team.

I reported to Charlie Company Commander, Major Donavan, and the company sergeant, Major Wales. We spent several minutes introducing ourselves to each other. I later learned that the detachment to which I was assigned had recently been created—and that all personnel on the A-Team were new members.

ODA 995 A-Team

I was happy to learn that all the team members had prior service in active duty and were experienced Special Forces soldiers. As I entered the Operational Detachment Alpha 995 (ODA-995) team room, I saw Sergeant Kelly frantically unpacking team equipment.

"Hey, Sergeant Kelly, my name is Sergeant Zapata. How are you doing? I am assigned to ODA 995 as the team sergeant."

Sergeant Kelly smiled and shook my hand, welcoming me to the detachment.

"Sergeant Zapata, I am glad you're here. The rest of the team members are eating dinner and should be back in a few minutes."

Sergeant Kelly brought me up to speed as to the team situation—its capability and equipment shortages and some of his other concerns. Sergeant First Class Kelly was of medium build, with sandy brown hair, and had prior active duty experience with the 75th Ranger Battalion and 10th Special Forces Group during operations in Bosnia and Croatia. He was Airborne Ranger and Special Forces qualified—and trained in communications, weapons, intelligence, and Military Free Fall High Altitude Low Opening/High Altitude High Opening (HALO/HAHO). I was happy to have a highly qualified man on the team. Sergeant Kelly was the senior Special Forces intelligence sergeant and also the assistant operations sergeant on the team.

Minutes later a Sergeant First Class Drum walked into the team room and introduced himself to me. Sergeant Drum was a tall, older man with a slim, athletic build and dark, black hair—a combat veteran with prior active duty experience as a medical sergeant with the 5th Special Forces Group during the Vietnam War era. Sergeant Drum was the most experienced senior Special Forces medical sergeant on the team.

Soon I had the entire team assembled in the room, and we were introducing ourselves to each other. Sergeant Marco was a man of medium build, with prior active duty experience as an engineer with the 10th Special Forces Group during the October 1983 terrorist attacks in Beirut, Lebanon SGT Marco was in Beirut when the 220 Marines were killed on October 23, 1983. Sergeant Marco would serve as the junior Special Forces engineer sergeant on our team.

Sergeant First Class Wilder—a man with a medium but athletic build, short red hair, and a freckled face—had prior active duty experience with the Force Recon Marines in Desert Storm, Bosnia, and Africa. Sergeant Wilder was the senior Special Forces engineer sergeant on the team.

Staff Sergeant Frank was slim and of medium build, with sandy blond hair, and had prior active duty experience with the 75th Ranger Battalion during the 1993 Somalia War conflict and also the 1989 invasion in the Panama War. Sergeant Frank was our senior Special Forces weapons sergeant on the team.

Staff Sergeant Brink was a tall, slim man with an athletic build and dark brown hair who had prior active duty experience with the 75th Ranger Battalion during the 1993 raid in the Somalia War conflict. He was Special Forces qualified in weapons and communications. Sergeant Brink was our senior Special Forces communications sergeant on the team and was our youngest soldier on the A-Team.

We now had a complete operational Army Special Forces detachment. We had multiple military occupational skills on the team, which made us a strong team, able to operate in a split-team concept if we had to. We had seven enlisted personnel on the team, minus a detachment commander. We soon would be getting a captain on the team within the next few days, before we began our individual team certification and evaluation.

Things started moving much faster during our second week. On Monday morning, we received our new detachment commander— Captain Cole. Captain Cole was a short man with a medium build who had been working for the Colorado National Guard in the Office of The Adjutant General (OTAG) as the nuclear biological chemical officer. Captain Cole had been able to get a release from his prior unit to enable him to participate with our unit during Special Forces certification and evaluation.

I later learned from the Charlie Company commander and company sergeant major that Captain Cole would not be able to deploy with us when the time came for us to travel in three weeks to Afghanistan. There had been some confusion on his orders—some errors in cutting the orders authorizing a certain number of soldiers from 5th Battalion, 19th Special Forces Group to go into Afghanistan. We would not be seeing Captain Cole until five months later in Afghanistan. However, Captain Cole's strong spirit and motivation kept him training with us during certification and evaluation until our Operational Detachment Alpha 995 loaded onto the C-17 aircraft and departed to Afghanistan.

During our second week of certification and evaluation and working together as a team, we spent a lot of time certifying on individual Special Forces basic common task skills. The days were long and tedious. We were now in our last week of certification, and we were spending long days and nights doing live-fire weapons qualifications with our assigned M-4 rifles and M-9 pistols.

We gradually began doing live-fire advanced tactical team maneuvering shooting scenarios, shooting at targets on the shooting ranges. We began executing team live-fire day and night ambushes, raids, and movement-to-contact scenarios on the shooting ranges.

We also spent long hours doing live-fire advanced urban operations, practicing building-clearing techniques and close-quarter battle shooting techniques.

I will always recall when our team was required to go through a live-fire semunitions exercise, using rubber bullets in a new urban mock city in a house-to-house hostile-streets scenario.

Semunitions were rubber bullets with colored paint inside the bullets. When hit by a rubber bullet, it was definitely painful—we noticed it when we were hit. All our rifles and pistols were converted to fire semunitions rubber bullets during this exercise.

The scenario was to simulate our A-Team going through an urban Mogadishu, Somalia, firefight while outgunned and outnumbered by the enemy.

URBAN COMBAT OPERATIONS TRAINING

The exercise was to test our skills in urban combat operations, our will to fight and operate under stressful conditions, and to learn how to control our men and seek cover and concealment during urban combat operations. It felt like running through a gauntlet shooting gallery, being shot at from all sides.

We practiced fighting against thirty personnel carrying rifles with rubber bullets, who were hiding on rooftops, in windows, and at corners of buildings waiting for us to enter the city. It was a chaotic situation, and we really never had a chance. Each team member was hit by rubber bullets three or four times just crossing a street intersection to seek cover and concealment. By completion of the training, we all had red, bruised skin on our bodies to remind us of the rubber bullets hitting us.

We spent two days on live-fire Special Forces basic and advanced demolitions training on the ranges. Training consisted of demolition breaching techniques, using det cord and cutting steel, with C-4 explosives, trinitrotoluene (TNT) explosives, and dynamite explosives. We set up and exploded claymore mines, set up anti-tank mines, and threw hand grenades. We fired the AT-4 anti-tank weapons, which replaced the old M-72-LAW anti-tank weapon, for weapons familiarization. We also familiarized ourselves with foreign weapons, such as Russian AK-47 rifles, RPK light machineguns, RPD belt-fed machineguns, and RPG rocket-propelled grenade launchers.

Our team had to plan and execute a live-fire exercise raid mission on a target during our final certification and evaluation test. We did not have any problem in passing this mission task.

Our last and final certification and evaluation as a team was to conduct an individual, time-recorded twelve-mile road march in full combat battle gear, carrying all weapons and other sensitive equipment and weighting our rucksacks at fifty-five pounds each. For those who know about military road marching, you know that your feet are torn, blistered, and in pain. Later, even your toenails begin to fall off. I was in great pain the next three days—as was everyone else. You never forget the pain and suffering you see around you after a twelve-mile road march.

The final certification and evaluation scores of all the A-Teams had been posted for review. We were eager to know which were the overall first-, second-, and third-place teams. As we reviewed the list, we were number five on the certification and evaluation list among the twelve Special Forces A-Teams going into Afghanistan. We were proud to know that we had done this well as a new team thrown together, in comparison with the other teams that had been working together for many years. It takes months and years for a new team to work together and function operationally. Many folks were surprised to see how well we had performed during the certification and evaluation testing. I was so proud of all the team members for their extraordinary efforts in working together as a team and passing the mandatory Special Forces certification and evaluation testing.

The only option we had in mission selection was to conduct Foreign Internal Defense (FID) in training the Afghanistan National Army.We were given a two-day pass to see our families for the last time before leaving. Our team members decided to have our last dinner together at Chili's Restaurant with all our families, so they could meet together for the first time. This also gave the wives a chance to get acquainted with each other and exchange phone numbers in case of an emergency.

On Saturday morning, we loaded onto an Air Force C-17 transport aircraft. We were on our way to Afghanistan.

CHAPTER FIVE

KMTC:
KABUL MILITARY
TRAINING CENTER

Our journey had taken us to our first stop at Rhein-Main Air Base in Frankfurt, Germany, for refueling of the C-17 aircraft. It took approximately an hour to refuel, and then before we knew it, we were in flight again toward Afghanistan.

The flight to Kabul, Afghanistan, took over four hours, and we arrived at Kabul Airport at approximately 3 a.m. The aircraft was flying tactical, with no lights, as it approached the runway. After landing, as we taxied, I tried looking through the port window to see what I could observe outside, but it was pitch dark. The aircraft finally came to a total stop, and the rear ramp door began to open. Immediately, an Air Force crew member signaled us to start unloading the aircraft.

I grabbed my rucksack and weapon and walked down the rear ramp exit. I could see other transport aircraft—and personnel loading and unloading cargo and equipment. It appeared that these transport aircraft were both German and French, loading their military personnel and cargo to depart from Afghanistan. I wondered for a moment if those soldiers had finished their tour of duty and were now returning home.

Finally, we were told to move to a certain location on the

tarmac till our 19th Special Forces Group representatives would come with vehicles to transport us to the Kabul Military Training Center (KMTC)—also known as the Special Forces Forward Operational Base (FOB). We had waited an hour before several personnel finally came with vehicles to transport us to our Forward Operational Base. It was approximately 4:30 a.m., and it was still pitch dark as we reached the Kabul Military Training Center and the Forward Operational Base main entrance.

As we approached the main entrance of the firebase, I could see soldiers from the 82nd Airborne working as the security force, carrying heavy crew-serve weapons as they provided security for the firebase. As we entered the KMTC and the FOB area, I could see concertina wire laid out along the entire defense perimeter. I also saw several sandbag bunker-fighting positions and observation towers positioned along the perimeter. Deeper into the firebase, I could see several three-story barracks. Some of the buildings were full of bullet holes or partially destroyed by rocket explosions. The bad smell of sewer shit and the stench of rotting human flesh stench hung in the air as we unloaded the vehicles.

We finally linked up with the representative who would lead us to our company assembly area. We were being temporarily placed in a large building until they could decide where to keep us later on. We started to unload some of our equipment, and by this time, we were tired and ready to get some sleep.

SCRAMBLING FOR COVER

Then suddenly, we heard an unbelievable sound. At approximately 5 a.m., we heard the menacing hiss of a bomb about to go off, then a loud deafening "Boom!"—the sound of an exploding mortar round or rocket hitting inside the Forward Operational Base (FOB). We immediately scrambled for cover, racing outside to our designated bunker-fighting positions. I heard a second and third incoming mortar or rocket round explode—hitting outside the KMTC firebase perimeter: "Boom! Boom! Boom!"

Our firebase immediately began firing illumination mortar rounds into the sky on the southwest side of the firebase. American forward observers had identified the possible location and direction of the incoming rockets. There were several high hills within three thousand meters of our firebase, and these hills were the suspected location from which the mortar rounds were being fired.

Within minutes the entire area was lit up with illumination rounds. We could see the surrounding terrain as if in broad daylight. I could hear 3RD Special Forces Group personnel shouting commands to the mortar crew, then immediately firing four to five high-explosive mortar rounds toward the suspected location of the enemy forces.

We quietly listened and observed—then heard our mortar rounds as they hit their targets in the distance: "Boom! Boom! Boom!" All we could do was sit and wait until further information and instructions came from our leaders as to what actions we needed to take in the event of a Taliban counterattack.

I remember communicating with each team member on our whisper radios to turn on their night vision goggles (NVGs), once the illumination rounds had ceased for several minutes. We were trying to see if there was any movement to our front. Shit! It was pitch black—we could see nothing within five meters in front of our fighting positions. During that night, had the enemy wanted, any of them could possibly crawled close to our perimeter. It was just too dark to see.

We continued to occupy our fighting positions until 8 a.m. before we finally got the order to stand down and safely return to our assembly area. Things were again normal for now. We continued to unload some of our equipment. I later learned that a Quick Reaction Force Team from the 3rd Special Forces Group had been sent out during the rocket attack to search and track the possible position from which the rockets had been fired. The team was not able to locate anybody or any signs of the enemy.

The Army 3rd Special Forces Group Airborne was the unit we would soon be replacing, and they were rotating out from the firebase. They still occupied their living areas, and we could not occupy those areas until the 3rd Special Forces Group had left the airbase to return home to the United States.

In the morning, we walked around the firebase to get familiar with the area. The morning was cold, but the sun was out, and we had clear skies. From where we were standing, it was a spectacular view. We could see the entire firebase and the surrounding high, jagged, and rocky desert mountains dusted with snow.

The Kabul Military Training Center (KMTC) was apparently an old Soviet Russian firebase occupied during the Russia-Afghanistan War. The Soviet Union had built Russian barracks and maintained personnel there, along with a large armored division of Soviet Russian T-72 and T-55 tanks. It was an eerie feeling to see how a powerful country such as the Soviet Union had just abandoned the area, leaving a large skeleton graveyard of tanks and other armored vehicles. A tall fence enclosed the compound, where all the Russian tanks and artillery had just been abandoned.

I could only imagine how it must have been during those days when the Soviet Union was fighting the Afghanistan Mujahideen guerrilla fighters in the early 1980s. I thought back to when the Soviet Union entered Afghanistan in 1979—only to begin withdrawing a decade later in 1989. I never dreamed I would be following in the footsteps of those Soviet soldiers here in Afghanistan.

Here we were now—American Army Special Forces soldiers getting ready to train the Afghanistan National Army. We were soon going into battle to fight the Taliban and Al Qaeda terrorists—and possibly the same Mujahideen guerrilla fighters once trained and equipped by the United States when they were fighting against the Russians. It felt as if we were repeating the same error the Russians had.

Within two days, the entire 3rd Special Forces Group had departed and rotated out from the firebase, and now our 5th Battalion 19th Special Forces Group Airborne was in command of the Forward Operational Base in Kabul. I noticed that we were sharing the KMTC firebase with a company-sized French Foreign Legion. The French Foreign Legion Army was also responsible for training the new Battalion Afghanistan National Army (BANAs) in everything from basic ceremonial drills to advanced infantry tactical techniques.

On our second day at the Forward Operational Base, our company commander requested a meeting with all company detachment commanders and team sergeants. The battalion commander and S-3 Operations had already decided which detachments would be conducting Battalion Afghanistan National Army (BANA) training. Our company commander relayed this information to us. All the other detachments were now tasked to train several Battalion Afghanistan National Armies. Once these were trained and ready for combat, we were to take them into a specific region and execute "confidence" combat missions.

ODA-995 GETS LEFT OUT

Our ODA-995 was not selected for this mission tasking, because our A-Team did not have a commissioned officer on the team. Instead, our detachment was selected and tasked to work in the Bagram firebase with the 20th Special Forces Group, Joint Operations Center, as liaison officers for the next thirty days.

None of the other detachments wanted to do this specific tasking due to its boring duty and the bullshit, fucked-up working conditions with the 20th Special Forces Group headquarters operations staff personnel. This meant working long, extra-stressful hours and different shifts during the day and night. This was going to suck. We discussed this mission tasking between our team members and decided that we would do the best we could until relieved from this duty position.

This was not what we had trained for as a detachment—to work only as liaison officers in the Joint Operations Center. Our team would be representing our 5th Battalion 19th Special Forces Group and supporting other Special Forces units already in the combat zone. Each member on the team would be working as a liaison officer for different units out in the field.

I had been tasked to work as the Joint Operations Center (JOC) non-commissioned officer. Our responsibility was to monitor all movements of the Foreign Coalition Forces and American Special Forces personnel in the combat zone. Twice a day—once in the morning and once in the evening—we were required to brief the 20th Special Forces commander and other generals as to the overall friendly and enemy situation throughout Afghanistan. This meant we needed to know everything the units were doing and what they needed out in the field.

Total two-way communication was required from the Special Forces Advanced Operational Bases in remote regions, in order to support them with ammunitions, food, water, emergency close air support, medical response, additional personnel, intelligence updates, and aircraft. In addition, these Special Forces units were busy sending live imagery information of Taliban and Al Qaeda targets back to our JOC for processing and preparation for future follow-on Direct Action Strike missions by other selected Special Forces teams.

Within a few hours, we were on our way as a team to Bagram Firebase to work as liaison officers in the Joint Operations Center for our battalion.

Sergeant Marco and Sergeant Zapata

(KMTC) Kabul Military Training Center Afghanistan

Graveyard of Russian T-55 & T-72 tanks

53

Russian tanks and BRDMs

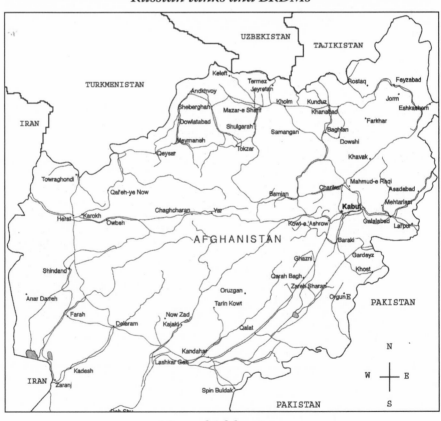

Map of Afghanistan

CHAPTER SIX

BAGRAM JOINT OPERATIONS CENTER

We had loaded all our equipment on four patrol vehicles to depart to Bagram. It was going to take us about two hours to drive from Kabul KMTC to Bagram Firebase.

Bagram Airbase played a key role during the Russian occupation of Afghanistan from 1980 to 1989, serving as a base of operations for troops and supplies. Bagram was also the initial staging point for the invading Soviet forces early in the conflict—and a number of Russian airborne divisions and Russian Special Forces units were deployed there. Russian aircraft based in Bagram provided close air support for Soviet and Afghanistan troops in the battlefield.

During the initial U.S.-led invasion of Afghanistan Bagram Firebase was secured by the British Royal Navy, their Special Boat Service being part of the United Kingdom Special Forces.

By early December 2001 U.S. infantry units from the 10th Mountain Division and soldiers from the 82nd Airborne Division shared the base with Special Operations forces and provided force protection at Bagram Airbase. All U.S. Air Force and Army aircraft based at Bagram Airbase provided close air support for U.S. forces and Afghanistan troops in the battlefield.

Before departing the firebase, we first had to get a Rules of

DESPERATE LANDS

Engagement briefing (ROE) from the S-3 operations section and an S-2 intelligence enemy situation update from our forward operational base. The entire team was briefed to stay on the hard asphalt-surfaced road at all times while traveling to Bagram. Hundreds of Russian explosive trap mines still have not been removed since the war between Russia and Afghanistan.

We received additional information about possible Taliban and Al Qaeda personnel placing Improvised Explosive Devices (IEDs) near or around roads used by the coalition forces and U.S. military forces.We began our departure from KMTC at 9 a.m., traveling in a northeasterly direction on a hard-surfaced road.

Though a nice sunny day with clear skies, it was cold. I was amazed to see for the first time how different things looked from outside the FOB and the Kabul city limits. I noticed the buildings—mostly mud brick homes—as well as the distant high mountain ranges, the varied terrain, and the types of clothing local men and women wore. The Afghan children just stared as we drove by. We could see a few camels grazing and roaming the open fields outside the city limits.

An hour into our travel time, we came to a narrow road in a canyon with high mountains on each side—a potential Taliban or Al Qaeda ambush location. As we moved deeper into the canyon, we saw on the left shoulder of the road two old Russian T-55 tanks and two large Russian cargo-transport trucks. It appeared that this equipment had been destroyed many years ago, when the Soviet Union was at war here in Afghanistan during the early 1980s. All we could see now were the rusty, skeletal steel frames of the armored vehicles rolled over on their sides. We saw several bullet holes in the equipment and, along the sides, much larger holes.

Our lead vehicle began to slow as we passed through this area. Suddenly, SFC Drum called me on our team's internal whisper radio.

"Hey, Sarge, did you see this shit? What the fuck do you think happened here to the personnel on these tanks and trucks?"

"Sergeant Drum, just keep fuckin' moving, dude—don't stop. All I can say is that the soldiers on these tanks and cargo trucks were maybe ambushed here by the Afghanistan Mujahideen guerrilla fighters during the late 1980s. It's a reminder to all of us, to see what these guerrilla fighters will do to us."

We kept moving quickly as we passed the destroyed armored vehicles, continuing a careful observation toward the low, flat terrain ahead as well as the high rocky mountains. One could only speculate as to what had happened here.

We were thirty miles from Bagram, when a left rear tire on our rear security patrol vehicle went flat. We had to stop the entire convoy to change the flat. Again, we were in a bad location, surrounding by rolling hills—an excellent potential ambush location. No other vehicles were traveling on the road. As I stood along the side of road for a few moments, I observed the surrounding rolling hills and the empty dry creekbeds nearby—and felt a cold wind blowing against my face.

An Ambush?

Suddenly, Sergeant Marco spotted the forms of five personnel moving at a distance to the rear of our Toyota gun-truck as its flat tire was being changed. Sergeant Marco—the M-240 machine-gunner on the gun-truck— immediately began yelling.

"I've got movement to our rear about 200 meters, moving fast in a file zig-zagging toward us. I see one person in the group carrying an AK-47 rifle."

Sergeant Marco began to aim his M-240 7.62mm machine-gun in the direction of the movement. The rest of us immediately got into a cigar-shaped formation—in prone firing positions around the patrol vehicles. As we continued observing, we saw the five personnel still approaching the vehicle but now walking slowly along the right side of the asphalt road. I was able to identify which one was carrying the AK-47. He carried the rifle slung around his left shoulder, which was considerably less threatening than had he been carrying it in the "ready" firing position. The rest of those in the group were not carrying weapons.

As they reached our location, they stopped about fifteen yards from us. We now were able to identify all five persons. They were young teenage kids who were curious, staring to see what we were doing. I yelled at Sergeant Marco.

"I'm going over—cover fire as I talk to them."

As I tried talking to them, they appeared smiling and affable. I was trying to figure out where they were coming from, but this was difficult because of the language difference. The kid with the AK-47 looked the oldest—maybe 17, I couldn't be sure—and he kept his distance from me. As I approached him, I was surprised to see his characteristic features and appearance. He had a white, freckled facial complexion, with red hair and blue eyes.

"Damn," I said aloud, "this guy must be a first-generation Afghan-Russian-born kid." He looked like a white Russian

I kept constant eye contact with the kid carrying the rifle. I also noticed that he was not wearing a load-bearing equipment harness with ammunition pouches or extra ammunition. I also saw that his AK-47 was decorated with colorful paintings on the front wooden hand guard and the rear wooden stock. The thirty-round magazine was also painted in different red, green, and yellow color stripes.

I tried talking to him by tapping my hand on my M-4 rifle and pointing at his AK-47. I wanted to know were he had gotten the rifle. He rambled on, saying something to me—but I was not able to understand a fuckin' word he said. Shit! For all I knew, he was a young farmer or hunter—or a young future Mujahideen fighter—and if I even tried taking away his rifle, he would most likely have fuckin' killed me for it.

I also wondered if maybe this guy was part of an advance group going around placing—or looking for potential locations to place—IEDs on the roads, or maybe setting us up for an ambush. Who knew? I reached into my cargo-pants pocket, where I was carrying a plastic water bottle, and gave it to one of the young kids. I received a happy smile in return. The kids were saying something to me, but I was not able to understand them. I then heard Sergeant Marco yelling at me.

"Let's go, Sarge—we are done. Let's get the fuck out of here—we are ready to go."

We immediately loaded onto our vehicles and continued moving again toward Bagram. We were now about five miles from Bagram and approaching our first Afghanistan Military Force (AMF) checkpoint. This was a security checkpoint the AMF had established for those entering Bagram. We saw three to four armed AMF personnel, carrying Russian AK-47 rifles and one light 7.62 x 39mm caliber machine-gun RPD, and a few Russian grenades—F1s with UZRGM fuse types.

As they saw our vehicles approaching, they waved at us. But we did not even stop—we just kept on driving through the checkpoint. As we entered Bagram, all we could see were several old, torn, mud-brick buildings. The main street to the city was crowded with Afghanistan people crossing the street. We continued driving through the main street, the Afghanistan people observing us as we drove slowly by.

Linking up With the Afghanistan Military Force

We finally reached the outer perimeter of the main entrance to the American Bagram firebase. The next checkpoint approaching was again manned by the AMF. The Afghanistan Military Force was a unit in transition to becoming an Afghanistan National Army soon. Until they could be organized and trained into a Battalion Afghanistan National Army (BANA) unit, they were not yet wearing full military uniforms but a mix of civilian and military clothing.

The AMF was part of the initial Afghan Northern Alliance Force— also known as the United Islamic Front (UIF)—that had worked directly with U.S. Army Special Forces personnel in fighting the Taliban and Al Qaeda forces since the beginning of the war in 2001, which started in northeastern Afghanistan.

They were experienced fighters, and some hated the Taliban or Al Qaeda organization. Some were former Mujahideen fighters and were perhaps sympathetic to the Al Qaeda cause. But as long as we paid them money, fed them, and armed them, they would be on our side helping fight against Taliban and Al Qaeda forces.

How did I know this? Well, because our team members and I would pick up money from the Civil Affairs Command in the City of

Kabul, and later on—once a month—we paid these guys American cash money to fight alongside us during combat missions.

We reached the main entrance to the American Bagram firebase, and for the first time we saw American soldiers at a security checkpoint. The famous 82nd Airborne Infantry Division was the security force at this checkpoint, and they inspected and searched every vehicle from top to bottom for any hidden IEDs on the vehicles before they could enter the firebase.

It appeared that the firebases where developed into multiple inner and outer firebase defense circles. The 82nd Airborne Division had control of the outer defense circle, and within that circle, the Special Forces Joint Operation Center had its own defense circle.

It took about forty-five minutes before we were released from the checkpoint to continue on to the Special Forces Joint Operation Center in the firebase. Once we reached the Special Forces firebase, we had to go through another security force checkpoint, but this time it was manned by Army Special Forces personnel providing the security around the firebase.

Entering the firebase, we saw three wooden buildings, several GP large Army tents, several parked Toyota gun-trucks, and Hummer patrol vehicles. As we reached one of the buildings, an Army Special Forces Command Sergeant Major Ivan introduced himself and said, "We have been expecting you boys. Get your personal equipment, and follow me to your tent."

He took us to the tent where we would be sleeping for the next thirty nights. As we unloaded our gear into the tent, he quickly took us to the operations center where we would be working for the next few weeks. After introducing us to the staff, he took us to visit the Special Forces Group firebase commander to hear more bullshit rules and policies.

For the next thirty days, the team would be working different shifts day and night as liaison officers for our battalion and other Special Forces units on the ground. Our duties were to monitor Special Forces personnel in the combat zone and assist them in coordinating any requests needed by the teams in the field. We would provide and coordinate the teams' emergency medical support, emergency close-air support, supplies, and other equipment. Whether we were working day or night shifts, it was always busy, and something was always happening out in the combat zone with Special Forces personnel.

I recall one late evening listening to the 'round-the-clock loud noises of a variety of U.S. Air force jet engines—from A-10 Thunderbolts to F-16s and C-130 aircraft—going out on emergency close air support missions. I could hear the constant loud sounds from the rotary blades of Army helicopters, flying out on various support missions and transporting troops on combat missions during our stay in Bagram Airbase.

Every day, I saw Special Operations forces, the 10th Mountain Division, and 82nd Airborne infantry personnel flying constantly in and out on missions from Bagram Airbase. The aircraft noise was nonstop. To this day, I still see in my memory these aircraft and hear their sounds as they took off on their missions.

Twice a day, morning and evening, we had to give a complete updated briefing to the Special Forces Group firebase commander and Joint Coalition Forces—on both enemy and friendly forces situations throughout Afghanistan. It was interesting to see other Special Forces personnel working as liaison officers—from Great Britain, Germany, France, Canada, New Zealand, Spain, Italy, and other countries. In addition to working liaison officer duty, we also had to pull security force guard duty on the Special Forces firebase perimeter.

NOT ENOUGH PERSONNEL—NOT ENOUGH SLEEP

This was slowly killing us because of our lack of sleep. We would average maybe two hours of sleep per day. I was fuckin' pissed off that Command Sergeant Major Ivan was not able to find additional security force personnel to support this tasking. In other words, we were pulling double duty, and it was affecting the morale of the team. But we continued to push on.

One morning at 3:30 a.m., we began to receive incoming insurgent mortar rounds or rockets, hitting outside the Special Forces Bagram Firebase. All I could hear were two loud blasts: "Boom! Boom!" I also heard a high volume of small-arms fire in the distance.

DESPERATE LANDS

We took our designated fighting positions around the firebase security perimeter. The 82nd Airborne Division security force immediately fired two illumination rounds into the air. I still was unable to see anything from my location. I began hearing on my radio of enemy information being passed along to each section leader, concerning possible insurgents probing the south sector of the special forces firebase. Sergeant Major Ivan had designated me as the section leader on the perimeter; therefore, I had to pass this information to each fighting position on my north-wall section.

Suddenly, another rocket round exploded closer to the south end of the firebase, and the low volume of small-arms fire began to fade away. I was trying to figure out where the shooting was coming from. It appeared that the 82nd Airborne security force had spotted three enemy personnel probing in their sector.

During the entire morning until 7:30 a.m., we were at 100 percent security alert, waiting for any attack from the enemy—but nothing happened. We returned to our normal duties as if nothing had ever happened. It was crazy! I kept saying, "Where the hell are these fuckers getting these rockets from?"

One late evening as we worked in the Joint Operations Center before giving our evening briefing to the commanders, we were scheduled to observe live footage of a Central Intelligence Agency (CIA) unmanned Predator drone aircraft executing a group of Taliban on a remote target. It was unbelievable to see the terror and horror this flying assassin could mete out.

As we watched the black and white footage on the screen, we could see the Predator aiming point system zero, focusing its crosshairs, and locking onto its targets. Those poor fuckin' bastards were ripped to pieces and did not even know what hit them. The killing was silent, fast, and accurate. The unmanned aircraft—flying above 10,000 feet—could not be heard or seen and was armed with two Hellfire missiles. Scary shit—not knowing, hearing, or seeing what is trying to kill you.

All of us stood there silently, with our mouths open, watching this whole operation go down live—but we were not the only ones watching the live targets and killings. An Army Special Forces team was near the targets and doing a live follow-up surveillance to confirm the killings, and later, to search the bodies and the area for intelligence data. It was a fuckin' nightmare come true for those poor bastards caught in the crosshairs. This, of course, would not be the last time we would see this killing machine working in Afghanistan.

On our fifth week at the firebase, we were already getting fuckin' sick and tired of doing liaison officer and security force guard duty. We were hoping to get someone to relieve us soon. Finally, our battalion sent several non-qualified Special Forces personnel to take over our liaison officer duties. We were ordered to return to Kabul Military Training Center (KMTC). We were glad to get the hell out of the Bagram firebase.

The following morning, we traveled back to KMTC in four vehicles. Two were civilian Toyota pickup trucks, and two were military Hummers. I had loaded—into the back of the Toyota pickup I was traveling in—personal equipment, our unit's mail, and several home-care packages.

We were the last truck at the end of the convoy. SFC Drum and I were sitting in the back seat of the Toyota. As we began driving out of Bagram Airbase, I noticed that the main street leading out of Bagram Airbase was very crowded with Afghans, forcing us to slow our vehicles as we drove through the main downtown street.

CHASING A THIEF

Suddenly, I heard SFC Drum yelling and screaming.

"Fuck! An Afghan has just taken one of our home-care packages from the rear of our truck and is running away with it! Stop the vehicle—I am getting out."

As I looked back, I could see the Afghan running. All I could say was, "What the fuck is happening?"

As, I looked back again, I could see that SFC Drum was already out of the vehicle and running full speed after the Afghan who had stolen the home-care package.

I turned around and told the driver, "Contact the lead vehicle to stop the convoy—and tell them we are on a foot chase in pursuit of an Afghan who has just removed some mail or a home-care package from the rear of our patrol vehicle."

Then I immediately began running down the street, following SFC Drums. As I kept running through the heavy crowd of people, I suddenly lost sight of SFC Drum. I found myself running through some smelly alleys near mud-brick homes and realized no one could know my location.

I used my internal team whisper radio to try contacting the lead vehicle—or anyone—to give them my present location and direction. Somehow, my radio was not working, and I unable to contact anyone.

As I continued running around behind one of the Afghan mud-brick homes, some of the Afghans in the alley were pointing toward something. I hoped they were pointing in SFC Drum's direction. But suddenly, I got nervous and suspicious as to what I might be getting into. All I could think was that I was perhaps being set up—sucked into a possible ambush I hadn't even thought about before beginning this chase.

As I continued running a few more yards in the direction the Afghans were pointing, I suddenly stumbled into a large, smelly, dry sewer hole. I finally located the Afghan, hiding inside a sewer shithole with one home-care package opened. Approaching the Afghan and looking down into the hole, my weapon was ready to fire several rounds into him. The Afghan boy turned his head in fear, facing me in shock, as he looked straight into the barrel of my weapon pointed at his face.

My finger was on the trigger, and I was ready to pull it, but I immediately stopped when I was better able to identify this person. The Afghan boy was probably in his early teens.

As I looked at the open package, I could see nothing but candy, cookies, and beef jerky inside. I could not believe that I had been getting ready to shoot and kill this kid for a box of fuckin' candy. Immediately behind me, several Afghan military personnel and SFC Drum arrived to assist me.

"Sarge, are you OK?" asked SFC Drum. "Did you get the home-care package back?"

"Yeah, I did," I replied. "Fuck, dude—I was ready to shoot this fuckin' kid for a box of fuckin' cookies and candy. Damn—can you believe this fuckin shit?"

I immediately recovered the home-care package and began looking to see who it belonged to. I could not believe what I was reading: the package had been mailed to me from my coworkers at the County of Santa Clara. To this day, I have never told them this crazy story.

I do have to say that working at the Special Forces Joint Operations Center as liaison officers was a valuable learning experience for all of us on the team. It gave us an overview and better understanding of how Special Forces were being used and what in actuality was happening in the Afghanistan battlefield. I guess this gave us an advantage over the other detachments from the battalion, in knowing how the system worked and how to find those able to assist us in the battlefield when we requested their help.

Within a few hours, we were on our way back to KMTC.

Special Forces Toyota gun truck with flat tire

Sergeant Zapata on security

Destroyed Russin T-55 tank

Second destroyed Russin T-55 tank

Afghan Military Force checkpoint

AMF security checkpoint

Downtown Bagram bazaar shops

Main entrance to American Bagram Firebase

CHAPTER SEVEN

TRAINING BANA INFANTRY COMPANIES

We reported to our company commander and sergeant major for an updated briefing on our new mission tasking at the Kabul Military Training Center. The Battalion S-3 operations and company commander had assigned us a team room, where we would be living for the next few weeks.

The team was also assigned two unreliable Russian UAZU-452 Jeep-style vehicles to help us transport our equipment, move around the FOB, and patrol the Kabul area. The vehicles had no armor protection and had been having constant engine failure problems.

Our detachment had been tasked to train two companies of a Battalion Afghanistan National Army (BANA). This was because all other battalion Special Forces detachments were busy in training other BANAs, and higher command wanted as many of these BANAs as possible ready for combat missions as soon as possible. Once these two BANA infantry companies were completely qualified and trained, our team was required to take them out and execute Combat Confidence Missions.

It was astonishing to learn and hear what our commanders' military political bureaucracy and policy views were in the past. The Commanders Military Policy would dictate which deployable teams would be going to Afghanistan and which teams would conduct direct action, strategic reconnaissance, or training of the Battalion Afghanistan National Army in Afghanistan.

I remembered our battalion's policy decisions—and its political bureaucracy and inefficiencies—when our A-Team had four months earlier been told in Fort Carson, Colorado, that we'd be going to Afghanistan to be used as support until our team commander arrived later from Fort Carson. In other words, we would continue to conduct support operations until our designated team commander arrived from Fort Carson within six months.

No Team Commander—and Other Challenges

Somehow, we had to figure out how to recruit some other young captain to be our temporary A-Team commander. Many young captains in the battalion were asking and volunteering to be the detachment commander for the team; however, battalion politics would not allow this to happen. This was a confusing policy on the battalion's part. I guess if it is not in the interest of the United States Army and higher command, then any policies or rules your commanders have told about in the past just don't matter.

Because of the Army's interests and these unique circumstances, we were going forward on our mission tasking without a team commander. Wow! I was surprised at this change of policy concerning our battalion. We were the only Special Forces detachment in the battalion without a team commander, and we found ourselves picking up the leftover shitty details from another detachment that had not completed training its two Afghanistan BANA companies. The bullshit lies and bogus reasons created by military command and given to young soldiers—as to why they might or might not have permission to do certain things—really amazed me.

We were going to train and pick up the worst companies from the Battalion Afghanistan National Army. The Afghanistan commanders were all either former Mujahideen, village chiefs, Al Qaeda, or Taliban fighters. Our A-Team had no way of really interviewing or screening each soldier prior to recruitment into the BANA. We had constant internal conflict between the tribal Afghanistan leaders as to who would be the next commander for their companies and battalions.

Some of these leaders were former village tribal chiefs and Mujahideen commanders who were recruiting personnel from surrounding villages to join the new Battalion Afghanistan National Army. The village chiefs promised the potential recruits that they would be paid, fed, and clothed by the Americans—and would serve under their own village tribal chief commander. This was a big problem because of traditional American military organization. American military structure provided only limited leadership positions for squads, platoons, companies, battalions, and brigades. The Afghanistan officers were required to rotate to positions with other units to get more experience and develop leadership skills.

So this was going to be a problem for all the Afghan commanders, because of the promises they had made to their village people in recruiting them into the Afghanistan National Army. The noncommissioned officer (NCO) corps in the Afghanistan BANA was nonexistent. We tried to build the Afghanistan enlisted NCO corps but had constant problems with lack of support from the Afghan officers. We constantly reminded the Afghan officers of the importance of having a noncommissioned officer (NCO) corps and of its doctrine.

As Army Special Forces advisors, we had to deal with this problem every day. We were also responsible to pay, feed, clothe, equip, and train the two infantry companies. The United States issued all the uniforms, boots, rucksacks, load-bearing equipment (LBE)—and all other equipment.

Russian or other previously Soviet Block countries donated ammunitions to the Afghan National Army. These countries donated new and used heavy and light weapons to them as well. The torn mud-brick buildings where the Afghan soldiers were living needed rebuilding because of inadequate electrical, water, and sewage systems. We had to provide bunk beds, heating stoves, and wood for the coming cold winter.

The United States somehow made some crazy deal and bought several hundred used Russian Kamaz three-axle transport trucks.

The United States also bought several Russian UAZU Jeeps that always had engine problems and were unreliable. The Afghanistan National Army in future operations would be using these same defective military vehicles.

We had soon begun a long, hard, and extraordinary journey in preparing these Afghanistan soldiers for combat missions. After our briefing with the Battalion S-3 operations and company commander, we returned to our assigned team room to discuss plans for how to start training these two Afghanistan Infantry Companies.

SFC Kelly would conduct basic intelligence training and wrote training schedules for the next several weeks. He also worked as the assistant operations sergeant. SFC Kelly was also a qualified 18E Special Forces communication sergeant and, with SSG Brink, assisted in providing communication training to the Afghanistan soldiers. SSG Frank provided all heavy and light weapons training, infantry tactics training, and coordinated issues of small and heavy weapons to the Afghan soldiers. He also coordinated the use of all firing ranges during live-fire exercises.

SFC Wilder and SGT Marco provided the basic training in different types of explosives, grenades, and mines. They coordinated all requests involving vehicle transportation to the field for the Afghan soldiers. They operated the supply section—and inventoried and issued all military uniforms and equipment for the Afghan soldiers. They were also responsible for building construction and remodeling of the BANA barracks and future firebases.

SFC Brink established all internal and external team communications and coordinated basic communications training for the Afghan soldiers. SFC Drum provided advanced and basic medical training and coordinated medical sick call every morning for the team and the Afghanistan soldiers.

B.S. Duty

I was stuck doing bullshit: officer staff meetings with both American and Afghanistan officers to coordinate equipment logistical support—and providing Army doctrine training and Army unit organizational structure for the Afghanistan officers. I also documented and prepared the payroll for the Afghanistan National Army with the assistance of SFC Kelly and SSG Brink. Finally, I assisted our team members in all training mission tasking when needed.

We had four Afghanistan interpreters, who would be going with us during our combat confidence missions as our translators. There names were Abdul, Kamal, Ahmad, and Amin. These interpreters were young Afghanistan college students paid for their services. A few had prior military experience working with the Russian military occupation during the late 1980s.

The interpreters would review and translate training schedules on a daily basis to give to the BANA company commanders. This was a huge task to perform and complete in time for the BANAs to review before training. The interpreters would also interpret all the training we provided to the Afghanistan soldiers—as well as our Afghan staff meetings.

One of our best interpreters, Ahmad, was a former Afghanistan Mig-17 pilot trained by the Soviet Union when Russia occupied Afghanistan during the 1980s. The story Ahmad told was that his aircraft was shot down by the Mujahideen with a U.S. Stinger weapon—a surface-to-air missile. Ahmad was injured and unable to fly again. He also shared with me some unbelievablly interesting stories of when he was a young pilot during the 1980 war between Mujahideen and the Russian military. He told me he was lucky to have survived the war.

One late afternoon when SSG Brink and SFC Kelly were at the Afghan Ministry of Defense (MOD) site with Ahmad, working with the Afghan infantry soldiers, they saw a German International Security Assistance Force (ISAF) Sikorsky CH-53 helicopter flying overhead—flames streaming from its tail. They watched the helicopter crash near one of the main roads leading into the city of Kabul. SSG Brinks immediately called the FOB to report the aircraft crash and its location.

SFC Kelly and SSG Brinks drove over to the crash site and were met by other British troops arriving at the same time. SSG Brinks and SFC Kelly tried to reach and rescue personnel from the helicopter, which was just behind a building off the main road. The helicopter had been on a routine patrol over Kabul and crashed in an area where many refugees lived. The rescuers could not get into the helicopter, because flares from the anti-rocket system kept exploding and going off. They also assisted in blocking traffic as they tried to reach the helicopter.

Unfortunately, all seven German peacekeepers died. It was first thought that two young girls had been killed by the helicopter crash, but they turned up a few hours later unharmed. SSG Brinks and SFC Kelly stayed on scene an hour or so to recover the German soldiers, then headed back to our FOB. Both SSG Brinks and SFC Kelly shared the gruesome story with the rest of our team members. This would be yet another heroic event unnoticed and involving team members from ODA995. We all continued our duties as if nothing had ever happened.

A Taliban Terrorist Strikes

The following day, the unbelievable happened, when two Army Special Forces members from our unit were ambushed on a routine patrol in downtown Kabul. Both SFC Marshall and SFC Leon were inside a Russian UAZU Jeep downtown during patrol, when a young Taliban terrorist threw a hand grenade inside their vehicle. None of the Russian UAZU Jeeps assigned to our unit had armor protection or window protection.

That day, the streets in downtown Kabul were heavily crowded and busy, with countless Afghans walking and crossing the streets. This forced their patrol vehicle to slow down, giving the attacker the opportunity to throw a hand grenade inside through the rear side window of the Jeep. Immediately, the hand grenade exploded inside the vehicle.

All that was remembered, from talking later to SFC Leon, was that he heard something loud hit behind the Russian UAZU Jeep. Then suddenly, the horrifying happened. Boom! An explosion went off inside their vehicle. Both men were thrown out of the vehicle and landed on the ground. Confused, they crawled, trying to reach their M-4 rifles for protection.

"I began yelling—screaming at Sergeant Marshall," SFC Leon said, "because I could see people moving closer around us and knew that the enemy was possibly returning to finish us off—so we had to get ready for another attack from the enemy."

First on scene minutes later were British and Afghan National Army patrols who responded to the ambush scene from just two blocks away. Within minutes, our unit and other American forces arrived on the scene to remove the men and the vehicle. Both wounded team members were transported to the German International Security Assistance Force (ISAF) hospital medical trauma center for treatment.

Both men had been seriously injured and received wounds to their heads, arms, and legs, and they were bleeding severely. Luckily, both had been wearing body armor—this gave them extra protection to their chest areas.

The young Taliban terrorist was captured and questioned by U.S. forces and the Afghan National Army. This would be another horrible event that would go unnoticed, involving American Special Forces team members from our unit. And again that day, we all continued doing our duties as if nothing had happened.

Every morning we continued to train the Afghan soldiers. Sergeant Frank—our Special Forces weapons and infantry tactics sergeant—had arranged two weeks of weapons qualifications requiring the Afghanistan soldiers learning to fire their AK-47 rifles.

On the third week, SSG Frank had the Afghan soldiers qualifying to fire heavy crew-serve weapons, RPD machineguns, 50mm mortar guns, and 82mm mortar weapons. Within several weeks both Afghan infantry companies were ready to do infantry company-size, platoon-size, and squad-size live-fire exercises on targets.

We had spent several weeks training the two infantry companies, and now their training was completed. Both Afghan infantry companies were ready to deploy for their missions. The Special Forces Combined Joint Task Force and the Forward Operational Base had decided on taking only one Afghan infantry company.

The command had decided on where the Afghan infantry company would be going to do their combat confidence missions. They would be going to Orgun-e Kalan Southwest, near the Pakistan border. The Special Forces Advance Operational Base (AOB) had enough room for only one Afghan infantry company in the firebase. Immediately, our A-Team and the Afghan infantry company prepared to depart for our new destination.

Issuing new RPD weapons

Cleaning new AK-47s

50-mm mortar gunner training

Mortar crew drill training

AK-47 rifle qualification

Afghan soldiers at the shooting range

New Afghanistan National Army

Chow time . . . food at the firing range

Afghan company at the range

BANA platoon marching drills

BANA tribal chief dispute

Team translators

BANA issued uniforms

SFC Wilder issuing boots

BANA waiting for equipment

BANA waiting for uniforms and equipment

CHAPTER EIGHT

ODA-995 FIRST COMBAT MISSIONS

In addition to training the new Afghanistan National Army, our team also conducted combat patrol operations outside the FOB surrounding area. This was because of prior night-time mortar and rocket attacks on the FOB.

On our second week back at the Forward Operational Base, the FOB had issued us a Warning Order and Rules Of Engagement (ROE) on our first team combat patrol. On their maps, the FOB had briefed us of the specific area to patrol, and the locations of both suspected enemy activities—and the areas of friendly forces. The FOB had also shown us our surrounding restricted patrol boundaries. We were required to stay within those boundaries due to logistical support and possibly friendly fire from the European Coalition Forces.

Our mission was to conduct a Mounted Security Force patrol movement in the surrounding Forward Operational Base until the next early morning. Several small villages that we had to patrol were located east and near the Forward Operational Base. This meant we would be driving around at night through nearby villages and setting up a security checkpoint on a busy road, looking for any illegal activity or personnel. The other option was to establish a surveillance site, looking for any suspicious vehicles or personnel moving near or around the Forward Operational Base.

DESPERATE LANDS

I immediately prepared and issued an Operations Order Plan to the team and one battalion S-3 operations officer who was observing the mission briefing. A total of ten Army Special Forces personnel were going on this mission: MSG Zapata, SFC Kelly, SFC Drum, SFC Wilder, SSG Frank, SGT Marco, SSG Brink, SSG Dale, SSG Black, and Captain Limb.

We were also taking two Afghanistan translators on the patrol—Ahmad and Kamal. In addition to the translators, we were also picking up ten Afghanistan Military Force (AMF) personnel. They would provide the additional firepower we needed on the patrol if their help was needed. I figured that if we had AMF personnel with us, our chances of being ambushed would be slim, due to the large military force we had. Having more personnel going on patrol with us gave me added peace of mind.

My thoughts were that in the event of an ambush, we would have additional firepower to mount an assault through enemy positions or help hold our position until further help came from the Quick Reaction Force and designated Emergency Close Air Support (ECAS) on call.

I was not going to take any chances. I knew we were going to be fresh meat for the enemy to try and ambush or catch, and we were definitely trying to draw the enemy out into the open. I guess you could call this "Movement to Contact" (MTC)—an operation to develop the situation and establish or regain contact with—and focus all efforts on finding—the enemy.

We took four patrol vehicles—two Toyota modified gun-trucks and two Humvee open-cargo transport vehicles. None of the patrol vehicles had any steel armor protection. They had been inspected by drivers SFC Wilder, SFC Drum, SSG Dale, and SSG Black. These were the only functional vehicles available.

SSG Brink checked our team internal radios—AN/PRC-148 MBITR radios and AN/PRC-117 radios—and setting up our frequencies and call signs, challenging passwords between the team and the Forward Operations Base. Sergeant Marco and Sergeant Frank inspected the two M-240 machine guns with their 8,000 rounds of 7.62mm ammunitions and mounted them on the gun-trucks' tripod stands. Everyone inspected and oiled their own M-9 pistols and M-4 rifles and carried a full combat load of several thirty-round magazines of 5.56mm ammunition—as well as several fifteen-round magazines of 9mm ammunition.

Each man carried at least one HE grenade; a smoke grenade; and several green, red, and white star clusters. SFC Wilder, SSG Brink, and SSG Frank were each carrying one M-18 Claymore mine for the patrol in case we needed to set up a hasty ambush. Each soldier checked and tested his personal PVS-7 night-vision goggles with extra batteries.

LEAVING ON PATROL

By sunset, we loaded all four vehicles and started driving through the main entrance gate and away from the FOB. Immediately, I could hear SSG Brink doing a radio check, notifying the FOB of our departure. We drove about a half mile and picked up the AMF Commander and his personnel.

Once we reached the AMF personnel, we met with the AMF commander, and I began to brief him on our mission tasking. The AMF commander also shared some important information, reporting that he had received complaints from several village personnel of an illegal checkpoint—with unknown armed subjects harassing the public—located east of a village called Buthkak, approximately eight miles southeast of the FOB. We found Buthkak on our maps and noticed that it was within our patrol boundaries.

As we looked at the map, we noticed a dirt road traveling west-to-east. We could also see a deep, wide creek traveling north-to-south along the dirt road near Buthkak. The map also showed some high surrounding mountains that would provide an excellent observation position for the Taliban. This location could also provide an excellent hiding site from which they could launch either mortar rounds or rocket attacks.

The AMF commander also warned that this area was a dangerous place, known to be very hostile toward surrounding tribal villages, European Coalition Forces, and American Forces in the area. We immediately discussed this information among the team members and decided to go forward and check out the area. SSG Brink immediately notified the FOB of our new destination and of the suspected illegal checkpoint east of Buthkak.

We loaded the AMF personnel onto both Hummer cargo vehicles. I noticed that the AMF personnel were carrying a mix of leather Mujahideen and American load-bearing equipment (LBE), with Russian AK-47 rifles and one light 7.62 x 39mm machine-gun RPD. Our order of movement on the mounted patrol was as follows:

Vehicle #1: Wilder, Zapata, Marco, interpreter.

Vehicle #2: Dale, Brink, interpreter, five AMF personnel.

Vehicle #3: Black, Limb, five AMF personnel.

Vehicle #4: Dikes, Frank, Kelly.

We continued driving on a dirt road, moving southeast parallel with a large, wide creek on our left. We began moving slowly south toward Buthka, in time disappearing into a black hole of darkness. We then began wearing our PVS-7 night-vision goggles (NVGs) to see better in the dark.

We now drove our vehicles with black-out head- and tail-lights. It was getting difficult to see the road and the vehicles behind us. Our patrol vehicles were moving tactically, trying to keep a good distance from each vehicle. The heavy dust and limited night visibility made it difficult to see how far apart the other vehicles were from each other. I felt weird—an eerie, helpless feeling—driving inside a vehicle at night on an isolated, dangerous road in the middle of fuckin' nowhere.

"How are you feeling?" I asked, looking over at SFC Wilder, the driver.

"Sarge," he replied, "it's pitch fuckin' dark out here—and I don't like this at all. This is fucked up."

Many dirt roads, trails, and creeks were not shown on the map, so we constantly rechecked our map to confirm the location of Buthkak and the illegal checkpoint.

Finally, we reached the outer city limits of the village. I did yet another map check to confirm our location before we changed the direction of our movement. Once we confirmed our location and direction, we continued traveling east on a dirt road away from the Buthkak. As we drove, we had to cross a large, wide creek flowing in the possible direction of the suspected illegal checkpoint. So far, everything seemed normal, and we had not yet come across any illegal checkpoints. We continued driving east for a few more minutes until we reached a small canyon with surrounding low, rolling hills. The road soon began to make sharp turns.

Approaching an Illegal Checkpoint

As we approached a right turn, we suddenly spotted what appeared to be an illegal checkpoint on the right side of the road, manned by three personnel armed with AK-47 rifles. The checkpoint appeared to be approximately 200 meters to our front.

We immediately stopped and communicated with each team member in the other three vehicles. Sergeant Wilder, our interpreter, and I dismounted from vehicle #1 and stayed behind the open doors. Sergeant Marco stayed on top of the vehicle with the M-240 machine-gun, aiming the weapon at the three subjects.

I felt nervous and could hear and feel my heart pounding harder—especially along the jugular veins in my neck—as we waited to learn what would happen next. My mouth started to feel dry as I continued observing the enemy.

I was somewhat confused by the situation at the moment and not truly sure what was happening in the surrounding area. My first thought was that the three armed men running away from their location were enemy decoys trying to make our entire convoy patrol move forward into some type of an ambush or something. My next thought was that the enemy might possibly be setting up an Improvised Explosive Device (IED) on the road. I was not sure, and I did not want to make any sudden moves forward that might get the entire patrol caught in an ambush on the road—whether nearby or farther along.

The initial plan was for the interpreter and I to continue moving forward by foot to identify the three armed men to determine what they were doing there. The remaining patrol vehicles also stopped, and their occupants began to dismount. Vehicle #3 and vehicle #4 immediately set up an overwatch firing support position on a small hilltop to our left rear. They were still able to observe the checkpoint with its three armed personnel—and our position—from their location.

Vehicle #2 occupants SSG Dale, SSG Brink, and five AMF personnel dismounted their vehicle. They also began to deploy on both sides of the road in an overwatch firing position in a line next to our vehicle #1, with SFC Wilder, SGT Marco, and me.

We could now see that the enemy personnel at the checkpoint were acting nervously and suspiciously. They immediately began running away from their position and up a steep, rocky mountainside. As they ran up the mountain about 200 meters, they suddenly stopped, turned, and appeared to be pointing their weapons directly toward our vehicles. The armed personnel continued moving quickly another 300 meters or so away from us. It was getting difficult to see them as they continued moving up the mountain.

ENEMY ON THE RUN

I could hear SGT Marco—our gunner with the M-240 machine-gun—yelling, "Those fuckers are going to shoot at us!"

He began aiming his M-240 machine-gun in the direction of the three armed men as they continued moving up the mountain like ground squirrels.

"Sarge, I'm going to open fire on them," Marco yelled.

"Can you see or hear them firing their weapons?" I replied.

"It's getting harder to see where the fuckers are moving," Marco yelled.

I told Sergeant Wilder to fire a white star cluster into the sky to get a better view of where the enemy was moving up the mountain. By the time the cluster opened and illuminated the entire area, the subjects had already disappeared up the mountain into the darkness.

I heard chatting on the radio—Sergeant Brink was communicating with the FOB, reporting our location and the situation we'd found—

a three-man illegal checkpoint. We communicated with the Bravo team—consisting of Vehicle #3: Black, Limb, an interpreter, and five AMF personnel; and Vehicle #4: Kelly, Drum, and Frank—that we were moving forward to the checkpoint.

Immediately, we fired another white star cluster into the air before moving. Once we reached our location, we again set up an overwatch firing support position. We again radioed the Bravo team to move to our location. As the team came closer to our position, they continued, bounding over through our firing positions. Bravo team moved up the hill by foot for several hundred meters in search of the three armed men. They were unable to locate them and returned in disappointment to our location. We had spent an hour searching for the enemy, but finally we decided to leave the area.

Somehow, the enemy had disappeared into the darkness, and they were hiding either in some secret cave or spiderhole that we could never locate at night.

Prior to returning to the FOB, we continued to patrol through several other villages. The farthest village we had to patrol was Tangi Kalay. Located about four miles due east from the FOB, Tangi Kalay was an easy drive—we just followed the hard-surfaced road. This was to be our last village to patrol. As we reached the city limits, we slowly moved around, looking for anything suspicious or unusual. It was late, and the downtown business market area was closed. I could see only a few people walking around town.

Once we completed our patrol in Tangi Kalay, we began our return to the FOB. Before arriving, we first dropped off the ten Afghanistan Military Force personnel at their location. We thanked the AMF commander for the hot-tip information on the illegal checkpoint—and for coming with us. We hoped that the enemy would not be setting up any other illegal checkpoints in the area or harassing the village people again. The AMF personnel seemed happy to have come along with us during the patrol. In return for helping us, we gave them two boxes of Meals-Ready-to-Eat (MREs).

Once we arrived back at the FOB, we debriefed the S-3 operations officer on our mission: the routes we took to get to the illegal checkpoint, and the actions we took at the scene. We also briefed him on any unusual activity seen in other villages we had patrolled. Once we completed our debriefing, we were released to return to our team room. By this time, it was already 4:30 a.m., and we were feeling tired and beat. We knew we had to wake up in just two hours to continue our mission tasking in training the two BANA companies.

The next morning at approximately 7 a.m., we were up again as if nothing had ever happened. We continued to prepare for training and meeting with the new Afghanistan National Army companies. This was certainly not going to be our last combat patrol operation in the area surrounding the Kabul Forward Operational Base.

Several weeks had passed as we worked inside the FOB, when our team was designated the Quick Reaction Force team (QRF) within the Forward Operational Base and Kabul Military Training Center. This meant that we were on standby for the next twenty-four hours to respond to any emergency combat support rescue operations required, to assist any American Special Forces units or European Coalition Forces on patrol who needed immediate help. Any units calling for assistance would do so because they had multiple casualties or injuries and needed medical trauma assistance—or extra firepower to help them fight the Taliban or Al Qaeda.

At approximately 11 a.m., the Forward Operational Base S-3 Operations had issued an operations order to our team, tasking us as the Quick Reaction Force. S-3 Operations again briefed us on the enemy situation, the Rules Of Engagement (ROE), and the restricted boundaries locations of all European Coalition Forces and America Special Forces units in the field. In the evening, I prepared and issued an Operations Order Plan to the team and the Battalion S-3 operations officer.

Our team quickly prepared and inspected all weapons, equipment, and vehicles required to execute Quick Reaction Force responsibilities if needed when the time might come. A total of nine Army Special Forces personnel were assigned, working as the QRF. The personnel were SFC Kelly, SFC Drum, SFC Wilder, SSG Frank, SGT Marco, SSG Brink, SSG Dale, SSG Black, and MSG Zapata. We were also taking two Afghanistan interpreters on the patrol— Kamal and Ahmad. This time, we were only taking three vehicles on patrol—two Toyota gun-trucks and one cargo transport Hummer.

It was now sunset—the time was approximately 10 p.m. Things were going quietly for the time being. This gave us some personal time to catch up on sleep, listen to some music, or write a personal love letter to our loved ones. Although there was not much privacy in the team room, we did the best we could to isolate ourselves from the surrounding people in order to have private time and a chance to do some personal thinking.

PACKAGES FROM HOME!

Receiving personal mail and home care packages was the most exciting time to all of us. I was always thankful when I received home care packages from several of my friends and coworkers at the County of Santa Clara Parks Department in California—and I especially enjoyed hearing from family memebers.

When receiving our care packages from home, we would always gather around like little kids, excited to see each others' care packages being opened and looking to see what was inside them. We typically received a variety of different nuts, home-made cookies, beef jerky meats, Doritos chips, and on special occasions, a bottle of Jack Daniels whiskey for us to share with everyone on the team—though this supply only lasted a few hours.

I will always remember when SSG Brink, the youngest man on the team, picked up our personal mail at the mailroom. He walked into our team room carrying our mail and a large box. SSG Brink was smiling—excited and happy about the package he had received from Vivid Company. SSG Brink had somehow been able to persuade a company named Vivid to send over some free porno-star DVDs. He explained to them that we were American soldiers in Afghanistan, and asked them if it might be possible for them to donate and send us some free porno DVDs.

Before we knew what SSG Brink had done, Vivid Company donated to our team one full box with fifty DVDs of their newest female porno stars. We were shocked and happy to have received this donation from the Vivid Company. Later, some relaxed and enjoyed reading personal mail, while other team members began to watch a DVD movie.

Suddenly, our company sergeant major walked into the team room to relay a message to me.

"Sergeant Zapata, S-3 Operations wants your entire team to report to the Operations Center ASAP. It appears that something has happened to one of our Special Forces teams from the battalion."

"Hey, Sergeant Major, what's really happening?" I responded, pressing for more details. "Where are these guys located?"

"Sergeant Zapata, I'm not really sure of the full details, but S-3 Operations will brief your entire team on the situation."

"Thanks, Sergeant Major. Tell operations we are on our way to the briefing room."

We all jumped out from our O.D. green, aluminum, folding sleeping cots, grabbed our weapons, and moved quickly to the briefing room. We sat in the briefing room looking at a large situational map on the wall. I could see other Special Forces team commanders and team sergeants in the briefing room also.

The battalion commander and the S-3 operations officer, named Major Sanchez, walked in to give us the emergency situational update on the American Special Forces team. This was going to be a large-scale operation calling for an entire combined Special Forces company-sized QRF operation to help the trapped team get out.

The situation was this: An American seven-man Special Forces A-Team from our battalion was out on an operation to remove suspected Taliban rockets and mortar rounds from an isolated remote ammunitions point twenty miles east of the Forward Operational Base. The information was that twenty Afghanistan Military Force personnel, heavily armed with AK-47 rifles and RPD machine-guns, were guarding and holding the ammunitions point. The American Special Forces team was there to remove all rockets and mortar rounds from the location. Information from an Afghanistan informant reported that rockets were being taken from the ammunitions point and later used to fire against the surrounding European Coalition Forces and American Forward Operational Bases.

What ended up happening was a firefight standoff between the Special Forces team and the Afghanistan Military Forces! The Special Forces team was not able to remove the rockets and mortar rounds, because the AMF had surrounded their vehicles and would not allowing the A-Team to remove anything from the ammunitions point. The Afghanistan Military Force threatened at gunpoint to defend the munitions and fight anyone trying to take any of the rockets and mortar rounds. Therefore, the A-Team was being held in the compound—surrounded and out-numbered by the AMF—and the team requested additional help.

Quick Reaction Force to the Rescue

Our battalion organized a large, combined, company-sized Quick Reaction Force to help recover the A-Team in trouble. We had a total of five Special Forces teams and ten headquarters company personnel. Sixty personnel total were involved in this operation.

A quick Frag Operations Order was given to all the teams by our designated company commander leading the operation. The Quick Reaction Force company quickly organized into three fighting elements—Assault, Support, and Security. Emergency Close Air Support was already notified and on standby. The assault element consisted of our team and three other Special Forces teams. The support element consisted of one team and ten headquarters company personnel. The security element consisted of one A-Team.

The order of movement to the ammunition point site was security, support, and assault elements. The security element was to secure the outer surrounding area of the ammunitions point. They were also going to block the entire west and east side of the asphalt road running in front of the ammunitions point, preventing any traffic from passing thru the area. This was a main road used for entering the city of Kabul.

The support element was going to occupy a location to provide supportive fire for the assault element—a small hilltop east of the main entrance to the ammunition point. The assault element took position near the main entrance of the ammunitions point.

At approximately 10 p.m., we left the FOB and began driving east to our destination. As we drove, I could see the long convoy of military vehicles moving quickly to their destination. And I could hear the communications chatter on the radio from the security element, informing the company commander that they were in position and ready.

Minutes later, I could also hear the support element informing the commander that they too were in position and ready. As we approached the ammunitions point, we took our designated positions within three hundred meters from the main entrance gate of the ammunition point.

From the assault position, we could see four AMF personnel at the main entrance of the gate. One appeared to be an officer and maybe in charge—but we were not sure. Both SSG Frank and SGT Marco were carrying M-240 machine-guns, ready to fire 7.62mm rounds. They were locked and aimed at the four subjects at the main gate entrance.

SFC Wilder also had his M-203 grenade launcher—ready to fire 40mm high-explosive rounds—locked and aimed at the building near the four AMF personnel. As we continued to wait, I looked to my left, observing the other two A-Teams on the assault element getting into a prone firing position, aiming their weapons in the direction of the ammunition point. All the other elements were in position, ready to execute the attack on the ammunition point. All we needed was the signal from the commander.

This was going to be a crazy nightmare if we had to assault up and through the main gate entrance, then up the dirt road to another building where other unknown enemy positions were located. Our company commander and company sergeant major both just stood there talking to each other.They appeared to be planning the best course of action before the release of all hellfire on the ammunition point.

Sometimes Diplomacy Is the Answer

Somehow, our commander wanted to talk to the American Special Forces A-Team and the AMF personnel at the ammunitions point one last time. The commander was finally somehow able to communicate with the Special Forces A-Team commander being held in the ammunition point. During the conversation, our commander requested to talk to the AMF officer in charge in the ammunitions point. An agreement was made between the AMF officer and our commander for both of them to meet in front of the main entrance gate of the ammunition point—right in the middle of the dirt road—to discuss the situation.

We could all see our commander walking slowly down the dirt road toward the entrance of the ammunition point, then meeting the AMF officer face to face in the middle of the dirt road. The problem was finally resolved between our commander and the AMF officer in charge of the ammunition point.

This was confusing for everyone to understand. The agreed plan was for the A-Team inside the ammunition point to leave all the rockets and mortar rounds—just leave the compound without anyone firing a shot or getting hurt. Arrangements called for a European Coalition Force from Spain to come with three cargo transport vehicles to move the American Special Forces A-Team out from the ammunitions point.

The Special Forces A-Team cargo transport vehicles were still loaded with the rockets and mortar rounds. The plan was to leave their vehicles there until the next morning, until higher American and European Coalition Force Command would resolve this issue.

The entire Quick Reaction Force company ended up staying in position until the European Coalition Forces from Spain arrived and transported the American A-Team safely away from the compound. By 2 a.m., we were back to the FOB.

I have wondered many times what might have happened if our company commander had not talked to the Afghanistan officer of the ammunition point. What if we had just attacked the ammunition point, with the A-Team still inside the compound? That night we lived to fight another day. Call it lucky—or call it good decision making.

We were now already in the month of December, and the two Afghan infantry companies had completed their training and were ready to deploy. The Forward Operating Base and the Advance

Operational Base in Orgun-E were requesting only one Afghan infantry company to deploy.

We were leaving within twenty-four hours for Orgun-e Kalan Firebase.

ODA-995 first combat mission operation

ODA-995 member test fires his M-4 rifle before going on mission

CHAPTER NINE

ARRIVAL AT ORGUN-E KALAN FIREBASE

The plan had changed. Our orders now were to take one Afghan infantry company and conduct combat confidence missions in the area of operations known as Orgun-e Kalan in the Paktika province along the border of Pakistan.

We would be executing confidence missions in the area of operations for a total of forty-five days, according to the information given to us. The politically correct phrase used from higher command was "confidence missions." Battalion operations had advised us not to use the phrase "combat missions." This meant that we—as Army Special Forces advisors—had to go out with the Afghanistan infantry companies and execute combat operations to test their capabilities, before allowing these companies to operate under their own command.

Missions to be executed would include raids, ambushes, checkpoints, search-and-seizure operations, cache-recovery operations, intelligence collection, and civil affair missions. As the senior Special Forces operations sergeant on the A-Team, I was busy requesting and coordinating transportation with our battalion S-3 operations center and the Army aviation units located in Bagram Firebase.

I had learned that already, two Army Special Forces A-Teams were in the Advanced Operational Base in Orgun-e Kalan. One of the

DESPERATE LANDS

A-Teams already in Orgun-e had been my old A-Team before the terrorist attack on September 11, 2001. I was the old team sergeant in charge of that A-Team before becoming the company operations sergeant. I knew well each member of that team and what their capabilities were. I knew they were a strong A-Team. I would be looking forward to seeing the old Team members again.

On my arrival, I knew they would inform me of the real situation there. The commanders in charge at Orgun-e Kalan Firebase were going to be Major Roberts and Sergeant Major Colon. I knew both men well from working with them in past operations. Both men would be facing difficult challenges in leadership capabilities in weeks to come.

I had to coordinate ahead of time with the commander in the Advanced Operational Base in Orgun-e Kalan, as to any special equipment or other logistical support requirements to maintain one Afghan infantry company plus an A-Team. The plan was to have three Army Chinook CH-47 helicopters scheduled to transport the infantry company and our A-Team to the designated Special Forces Advanced Operational Base located ten miles from the border of Pakistan.

A BAD-WEATHER DEPARTURE

Departure day arrived the morning of December 24, 2002 at approximately 8 a.m. One Afghan infantry company and one Army Special Forces A-Team awaited transportation from the Kabul Military Training Center helicopter landing zone.

As I looked around that morning, the weather was cloudy, windy, snowing, and cold. The surrounding buildings and the nearby rolling terrain and more distant high mountains were white because of the heavy snow falling. The beauty and peacefulness of the surrounding high, jagged mountains covered in white snow provided an amazing view as the snow continued to fall.

Because of the number of personnel transported, the Army Chinook CH-47 helicopters would be making four separate lifts in transporting one Afghan infantry company—a total of 120 Afghan soldiers—and seven American Army Special Forces A-Team personnel with all our personal and tactical equipment. The helicopters had limited space—and limits on the weight they could carry in personnel and equipment.

I had to organize all personnel into separate groups, placing them into four lifts with thirty personnel per lift on each aircraft. This included weapons, rucksacks, and ammunition boxes, and two large GP tents with personal and sensitive equipment. I knew we were going to be over the required space limit on the aircraft, but we continued to stage all our equipment at the landing zone.

A few days prior to our departure, the Afghan infantry company soldiers were busy as bees loading, packing, and inspecting all their personal and tactical equipment. This included all light and heavy crew-serve weapons, Russian AK-47 rifles, RPD machine-guns, 50-mm mortars, and 82-mm mortar weapons. The infantry company would be taking several live ammunition crates of Russian 7.62 x 39mm munitions, 50-mm mortar rounds, 82-mm mortar rounds, explosives, and meals-ready-to-eat (MREs) required for our missions for the duration of the time in the area of operation.

Our A-Team had also inventoried and inspected all our own team's required tactical equipment—radios, weapons, ammunition, rucksacks, and other personal equipment. I right away prepared an aircraft flight manifest of all personnel boarding the helicopters. The manifest was always a requirement in order to identify what personnel were aboard which helicopters. In the event of a crash or other unforeseen event, this would help in identifying bodies.

I gave a copy of the aircraft flight manifest to the Departure Air Control Commander (DACO), Battalion Operations Center—and to the aircraft pilots—for their record keeping. Each group on the lift would have at least one Army Special Forces advisor within the group during the flight to our destination.

This is how each group and lift was broken down per aircraft:

▶ Lift #1 was SFC Drum, SFC Wilder, and thirty Afghan infantry soldiers with all their equipment.

▶ Lift #2 would be SSG Frank, SSG Brink, and thirty Afghan soldiers.

▶ Lift #3 would be SFC Kelly, SGT Marco, with thirty Afghan soldiers.

▶ Lift #4 would be thirty Afghan soldiers and myself, with all other required equipment.

As we staged at the landing zone in the morning, we awaited the arrival of three aircraft. Several minutes had passed, and I could hear at a distance the Departure Air Control Officer talking over the radio with personnel from Bagram Firebase as to the status of the requested three aircraft coming to our location.

A Change of Plans

Suddenly the plans changed. We now had two Army Chinook CH-47 helicopters coming to pick us up. One of the other helicopters had engine problems and would not be flying. Nothing would be changing in our groups and lifts—the only issue now was that it was going to take us longer to get to our destination with just two helicopters.

I could see that weather conditions were beginning to worsen. The skies were looking inreasingly dark and gray. Visibility was getting even worse, with the snow falling. My concern was the possible cancellation of the aircraft because of reduced visibility. Suddenly the Departure Air Control Officer (DACO) yelled and said, "Sergeant Zapata, the helicopters are five minutes away and coming in fast. Get your people ready now!"

Those on lifts one and two began adjusting their equipment one final time before preparing to load the helicopters. I looked to my left side and saw the emotions and excitement SFC Drum, SFC Wilder, SSG Frank, and SSG Brink expressed as they grabbed their rucksacks and personal equipment. Before I knew it, I heard the sound of the rotary helicopter blades from the helicopters growing louder as they drew closer to the landing zone. As I looked up into the sky, I could see two storm-trooper warship aircraft approaching fast toward the landing zone.

Both helicopters hovered over the landing zone and then landed a good distance apart, without shutting the engines off. Their rear ramp doors opened and lowered, and inside, we could see three Army crew chiefs wearing flight helmets. They were dressed in desert flight suits, walking on the rear ramp, and waving to both lifts to start loading immediately.

Our personnel began to load all their equipment onto the aircraft and began adjusting the boxes and rucksacks on the aircraft floor. The men then quickly took their places on the red-netted seats. Once all the seats were full, they began sitting in the middle of the floor, on the tops of rucksacks, boxes, equipment—wherever they could find a place to sit. Both aircraft were full, and no more space was available. We were packed in like cattle.

Suddenly the rear ramp doors of the helicopters started to close, and I heard the sound of the engines and rotary blades growing louder, pushing the wind against my face. I could see Drum, Wilder, and Brink, and Frank giving me a final wave and thumbs up as the ramp door closed. The helicopters started to move upward and started flying away to their new destination.The flight time to Orgun-e Kalan, Advanced Operational Base would be one hour. Once the aircraft unloaded their personnel there, they would return and pick up the rest of our group here at KMTC.

An hour had passed, and the Departure Air Control Officer was communicating with Orgun-e Kalan as to the status of the Chinook CH-47s. Both aircraft had arrived safely and were refueling. But by now the weather at Orgun-e Firebase had grown even worse. Visibility was bad because of heavy snow and low, overcast clouds. The aircraft would not be flying back again until weather conditions cleared up sometime tomorrow morning.

Weather conditions in our area too began to worsen. We decided to move the two Afghan platoons into a building next to the landing zone. We would have to wait until tomorrow morning to stage again at the landing zone for another pickup.

MERRY CHRISTMAS TO US

The next morning—Christmas Day, December 25, 2002, at 8 a.m.—two Afghan infantry platoons and three Army Special Forces A-Team members were again awaiting transportation at the Kabul

Military Training Center helicopter landing zone. Weather conditions were now much better than they had been the day before, but it was still cold and sunny, with some scattered clouds. Visibility looked clear and good for flying.

I began looking at the surrounding high, jagged mountains covered in white snow. This time, I had an awful, eerie feeling about the surrounding mountains. It felt as if they might *look* peaceful, yet somehow be dangerous and threatening to us. Both our groups began staging near the landing zone, waiting for the aircraft to arrive. It was now 9 a.m., and I could hear the Departure Air Control Officer (DACO) talking to the pilots at the Advanced Operational Base on the status of their arrival at the KMTC landing zone.

Several minutes had passed, when the Departure Air Control Officer turned and looked at me with a serious look on this face. But then he smiled as he gave me a thumbs-up and said, "Sergeant Zapata, the aircraft are eight minutes away—get your men ready."

"Yes, Sir," I replied. "Thanks."

I relayed the information to SFC Kelly and SGT Marco, who were on Lift #3. I also relayed the information to Lift #4, my Afghan platoon. Within minutes, we heard the distinct sounds of the CH-47 helicopters' engine props and rotary blades growing louder. Then the two giant storm-trooper warship aircraft pulled into view, hovered over the landing zone, and landed a distance apart from each other—without shutting the engines off.

As before, we saw the rear ramp doors opening and lowering. I could see three Army crew chiefs from the aircraft walking on the rear ramps, waving to both our lifts to start loading. Our personnel began loading all our equipment and adjusting the boxes and rucksacks on the floor, but this time the red, netted seats stayed folded upward to give us more room for seating on the floor.

Personnel began to sit in the middle of the floor, on the tops of rucksacks, boxes, equipment—and wherever they could find a place to sit. The rear ramp doors started to close, and I heard the increasing noise of the engine props and rotary blades pushing against the wind.

Looking around inside the aircraft, I saw the two crew chiefs taking their positions next to the front two-sided open window exit ramps. On the edge of both the left and right window ramps were mounted two M-240 machine-guns on tripod stands. Within minutes, we were in the air and flying to our destination. Flight time to our destination was one hour.

We had been flying for a few minutes when I decided to look at my topographical map, to get a general idea as to our route during the flight in case of an emergency or unexpected development. As I looked at the map, I could see that we were going to fly over some high mountain ranges. The mountain elevations were from as high as 9,000 feet to as low as 6,000 feet. We would be flying thru some deep, narrow canyons and valleys to get across the mountain ranges in order to reach the Advance Operational Base near the border of Pakistan.

As I sat near one of the opened exit window ramps, I could see the approaching rugged snow-covered mountain ranges with their sharp peaks, deep canyons, and valleys—an almost impenetrable barrier for anyone on the ground. The surrounding terrain had no vegetation—just mixed snow, rocks, and dirt. By checking my topographical map, I oriented myself as to our location and direction we were flying.

On Approach to Orgun-e Kalan

Several minutes passed, and one of the crew chiefs came up to me and said, "We are six minutes away from arrival to Orgun-e Kalan firebase."

I gave the crew chief a thumbs-up to acknowledge his information. I then turned and passed the information to the Afghan soldiers on the aircraft. Within minutes, I felt the helicopter ride getting bumpy and noticed it making a sharp right turn. During the turn, I could see through the window—at a distance—the entire Orgun-e Kalan Firebase below. We were now flying into a small open valley with nearby surrounding rugged mountains

I noticed too that the construction of the firebase was in a unique triangle shape—built this way as a defense measure. This defense technique would provide a 360-degree view for fire protection if the firebase were ever under attack. As we got closer, I spotted at a distance two AH-64 Apache Attack helicopters flying near and around the firebase in a figure-8 pattern, resembling two vultures hunting for their prey.

It appeared as if the helicopters were looking for something or someone. They would move from one location to another, quickly hovering over a certain mountain range like a buzzing bee searching for honey. I could see a small landing zone inside the perimeter of the firebase—and parked on the zone were an AH-64 Army Apache attack helicopter and four UH-60 Army Blackhawk helicopters.

I could also see several other unknown personnel standing near the landing zone with several transport vehicles. Our aircraft started to hover over the landing zone, then landed safely within the firebase. The engines were kept running as the rear ramp door started to lower. As the door lowered, I saw the second helicopter behind us, hovering like a giant bee and landing a distance from us. The crew chief began motioning for us to start unloading the aircraft. We began picking up all our equipment and personal effects and headed out of the aircraft.

As I stepped off the rear ramp of the helicopter, I saw Drum, Frank, Wilder, Brink, and other Afghan soldiers approaching both aircraft to help us unload equipment and quickly move some of our A-Team equipment and personal equipment to our tents.

I could see, as SFC Drum and SFC Wilder approached the helicopter, big smiles on their faces.

"It's about time you guys got here," said SFC Drum. "What the hell took you guys so long to get here?"

"Sarge, you are going to love this fuckin' shit-hole place," added SFC Wilder. "This place is fuckin' unreal."

"Alright," I replied, "but tell me about it later after we get to our team room."

The A-Team equipment was for the time being stored in a building occupied by another A-Team that was leaving the next morning. Meanwhile, our A-Team would be staying in a large Army GP tent with no heating system. We had plenty of Army sleeping cots to sleep on but no heat—and it was cold.

SSG Frank was busy escorting the other two Afghan platoons to the area where they would be staying with the entire Afghan company. The Afghan company would be staying inside a large structure and using several Army tents.

As I unpacked my personal equipment, Master Sergeant Moons—the new team sergeant from my old A-Team—came over to shake my hand and said, "Sergeant Zapata, it's good to see you again."

"Hey," he continued, "your team can move into our building tomorrow morning as soon as we empty it out, because our team will be leaving then."

A Taliban Encounter

MSG Moon then began to share an incident involving his entire A-Team which had gotten his team into some trouble with the Advanced Operational Base Commander. Moon said they were on a routine patrol two days earlier, flying on an Army Blackhawk helicopter along the border of Pakistan. The helicopter pilot spotted five Taliban personnel—carrying two RPGs and AK47 rifles—crossing the rugged mountain border into Pakistan.

The helicopter pilot commander and the A-Team commander decided to land the A-Team in Pakistan territory to intercept the Taliban personnel. The Taliban had been sighted on a trail moving toward a nearby abandoned, torn mud-house. Here, the team planned to set up a hasty ambush and wait for the Taliban.

Somehow, the Taliban deviated and took a different route, escaping across the Pakistan border. The helicopter pilot reported observing from the air a platoon-sized Pakistan force at a border checkpoint. The Pakistan forces allowed the Taliban forces passage without any challenge or search of the equipment the Taliban were carrying.

The Pakistan forces had observed the American helicopter landing in Pakistan territory. The Pakistan forces could also see the unloading of the Army Special Forces team near an abandoned mud house. The Pakistan force immediately began to move toward the ambush location. The Pakistan force deployed into a combat formation, prepared to engage in a fire-fight with American Army Special Forces personnel.

Luckily, another American Army Special Forces officer had seen the American Blackhawk helicopter drop off the Special Forces team in Pakistan territory. The American officer and other men were on a surveillance mission near the area. They knew the Pakistan platoon commander and were able to deescalate the whole incident, preventing it from becoming a big fire-fight between U.S. forces and Pakistan forces.

Therefore, MSG Moon's team was in trouble for taking action in chasing the Taliban and entering Pakistan. The team had to return to the FOB for an investigation on the incident. The next morning MSG Moon and his team were loading one Chinook CH-47 helicopter and flying back to Kabul FOB.

All I could tell MSG Moon was that I probably would have done the same thing if I'd been in his position. It was a crazy situation under the circumstances. His team was doing their job in chasing the enemy to destroy it. He shook my hand and said good luck. I was continuing to unload some of my equipment, when one of the AOB staff members walked into the tent to inform me of my meeting time with the AOB commander. My first meeting with the commander was set for the next morning.

Meanwhile. SFC Drum was going to give me a quick orientation to the area and introduce me to some of the other A-Teams at the firebase.

ODA-995 team members at KMTC landing zone—24 Dec. 2002

KMTC helicopter landing zone—24 Dec. 2002

*MSG Zapata with interpreter and Afghan platoon
at KMTC landing zone on 25 Dec. 2002*

Loading Afghan troops on Chinook CH-47 helicopter

Army Chinook CH-47 helicopter arriving at KMTC—
25 Dec. 2002

MSG Zapata flying to Orgun-e Kalan Firebase—25 Dec. 2002

Interpreter with Afghan platoon—25 Dec. 2002

MSG Zapata, with old A-Team members in Orgun-e Kalan

A-Team with Afghan Military Force in Orgun-e Firebase

CHAPTER TEN

COMBAT CONFIDENCE MISSIONS SAROBI

On the second day at Orgun-e Kalan Firebase, I had to meet in the morning with the Advanced Operational Base commander, Major Roberts—and Sergeant Major Colon—to receive an enemy and friendly forces situational update briefing of the area of operations.

In addition to receiving the situational briefing updates, the AOB commander and sergeant major lectured me on safety and their policies and procedures while on the firebase. The AOB commander also asked me for our team's status—and the readiness status of the Afghan infantry company we had brought to the firebase.

During the commander's briefing I had learned that the AOB had an infantry company from the 82nd Airborne Division working as the security force at the firebase, with three attached Army Apache attack helicopters and three Blackhawk helicopters, with their pilots, assigned to the AOB. I quickly learned that a second Afghan infantry company was working with another A-Team from one of the other companies on the firebase.

I knew well who the team commander, team sergeant, and team members were. In addition to the A-Team from Alpha Company, a second A-Team from Charlie Company was assigned to the AOB. I also knew their team commander, team sergeant, and team members.

DESPERATE LANDS

Both A-Teams from Alpha and Charlie Companies were excellent teams and capable of executing any difficult mission tasking given to them. They were some serious boys, focused on succeeding in their missions. Also assigned to the AOB were members from the United States Army Civil Affairs and Psychological Operations Command (USACAPOC). The U.S. Army 351st (CA) Civil Affairs unit had a five-man team, and the 4th Psychological Operations (PSYOP) Group unit had a five-man team attached to the AOB.

At the end of our briefing, Major Roberts issued me a Warning Order on a Medical Civil Affairs and PSYOP operation located in a village called Sarobi. I was to plan and execute this mission tasking with five other Civil Affairs and PSYOPS personnel the next morning.

After my completed briefing with the AOB commander and the sergeant major, I returned to our team room to inform my team members of the AOB commander's Policy and Procedures—and of the enemy and friendly forces situation in the Area of Operations, to include the warning order on the Medical Civil Affairs mission for the next morning.

The rest of the day was spent getting orientated to the firebase and checking out the surrounding firebase security perimeter and fighting positions. We continued to check in with the Afghan Company we had brought to the firebase, to see how they were getting settled.

Each of our detachment members was assigned to a designated Afghan platoon, in order to monitor and better control the Afghan company requirements. Throughout the day, our team members continued to coordinate with and assist the Afghan company on mission preparations and firebase work priorities.

The Afghan soldiers had set up their tents and were happy talking to the other Afghan company soldiers who had recently arrived just two weeks ago. As I spoke to our Afghan company commander, he was eager to start patrols and to get into the battlefield. I issued him the Medical Civil Affairs mission tasking.

The plan was to take two Afghan platoons from his company for this mission. I wanted him to select two of his best platoons to go with us on this operation. The Afghan platoons were organized into assault, support, and security elements to operate while we were in Sarobi during our meeting with village chiefs and warlord commanders. The platoons' main function was to provide security while we were having our meeting with these village warlord commanders. They were to conduct cache searches of any weapons, ammunitions, and explosives within the compound.

THE VILLAGE WARLORDS

The information we had on the village warlords was that they had a fortified firebase with over ten personnel, heavily armed and equipped with a Chinese Type-75 anti-aircraft machine gun. The Chinese anti-aircraft machine gun was a single barrel, fired 14.5-caliber rounds and was located on top of a building. The weapon had complete 360-degree-visibility field of fire on any target approaching their compound. The weapon would be a threat to any aircraft flying near the village and to any armored vehicles or ground forces approaching the firebase.

Many questions were asked on how the village warlords had been able to get this Chinese Type-75 anti-aircraft machine gun and why was it located on top of a structure controlled by the Sarobi warlords. For the moment, all I wanted the Afghan company commander to do was to get orientated to the area and to prepare his men for the mission coming up the next morning. I had given him all the detailed information he needed to prepare for the mission.

As I departed the Afghan security perimeter, I noticed that the two Afghan companies had built another internal security perimeter wall within our own firebase. It was interesting to see this technique used on a defense security perimeter within the firebase.

Both Afghan companies on the firebase were also responsible for providing twenty-four-hour security force protection on the firebase, to include working as a Quick Reaction Force (QRF) if needed. The Afghan company had to prepare and schedule a rotating guard roster shift while on the firebase.

Later that afternoon SSG Frank and I began to inspect and familiarize ourselves with each Afghan security perimeter fighting position and observation point within the surrounding firebase. The Afghan security perimeter and fighting positions were built well. As we completed our inspection, we continued to walk around and inspect also the entire designated American security perimeter and fighting positions.

I noticed that soldiers from the 82nd Airborne Division occupied each fighting position and observation point within the surrounding firebase. Two American soldiers occupied each fighting position at all times. In the center of the firebase were located six mortar-gun fighting positions from the 82nd Airborne Division. The American enlisted soldiers were inspecting and cleaning their mortar guns. They continued to improve their fighting positions by filling sandbags and building a mound of dirt to be used as a protective barrier.

By the time we completed our perimeter security check on the firebase, it was dark and late. The night was growing extremely cold. It reminded me of the extreme cold weather in Alaska during winter nights. SSG Franks and I decided to return to the team room to check in with the rest of the team members. It was 9 p.m., and we began our team meeting to discuss what we had seen thus far within the firebase and to share any concerns or problems that needed cared for before the end of the night's business. We completed our team meeting and were happy with the results, so we decided to get some sleep to be ready for tomorrow.

The next morning at 8 a.m., I gave an operations order to my detachment—the Civil Affairs, PSYOPS members, and the Afghan company commander—prior to our departing the firebase.

Our emergency close air support would be provided by AH-64 Apache attack helicopters coming from Orgun-e Klan Firebase. Our order of movement as a unit to Sarobi was as follows:

▶ Vehicle #1—SFC Drum, SSG Brink.

▶ Vehicle #2—SFC Wilder, MSG Zapata, SGT Marco.

▶ Vehicle #3—SSG Frank, Afghan interpreter, and thirty Afghan soldiers on a Kamaz transport truck.

▶ Vehicle #4—SFC Kelly, Afghan interpreter, and thirty Afghan soldiers on a Kamaz transport truck.

▶ Vehicle #5—five enlisted personnel from the Civil Affairs and PSYOPS Team.

A total of five vehicles and seventy-four military personnel were going on this mission to Sarobi. Our A-Team was tasked to execute a Medical Civil Affairs and PSYOPS operation in Sarobi. The village was ten miles northwest of the Pakistan border and eleven miles southwest of our Orgun-e Kalan Firebase.

Our mission would be to meet several village chiefs and warlord commanders in Sarobi. We would be providing patient care, medicine, medical equipment, and other supplies for their village hospital. Our Special Forces team medics would provide primary care medical attention to the village patients if required.

We were to discuss with the village warlord commanders any future construction requests they might need for building a water pump, water storage site, or a medical clinic to serve nearby villages. Another mission task was to convince the local population of the surrounding villages to support American troops in their Afghan and U.S. policy and national objectives. During my meeting with the village chiefs and warlord commanders, I was to collect any other information about Al Qaeda or Taliban movements in the Area of Operations.

By 9 a.m., our patrol was leaving the front entrance of the firebase, headed for Sarobi. The morning was cold and overcast. You could see the surrounding high mountains covered with snow. I heard SSG Brink—our team radio operator—doing a radio check and notifying the Advanced Operational Base of our departure, as we drove past the main gate.

After driving on a muddy, wet road for an hour, we approached a small village, and I was able to see several adobe mud homes with children standing near the road observing us as we drove by. Some of the children looked ill and poorly dressed. I saw some with dirty faces and no shoes. Some smiled—and some just stared in amazement as we drove by.

We were now approaching the outer city limits of Sarobi, and I could see the large warlord compound at a distance. The compound was located on a ridge overlooking the entire surrounding valley. I noticed that the compound had high adobe mud walls surrounding it, protecting an interior courtyard. Four watchtowers were located on each corner of the compound walls.

We were now approximately a thousand meters away from the compound. Suddenly, the lead vehicle communicated over the internal team radio to advise that they were stopping to view our target better. The first thing SFC Drum and SSG Brink communicated was visual sighting of the Chinese Type-75 anti-aircraft machine gun, perched atop one of the towers at the southeast corner of the compound. They continued to report, noting that they could see a gunner and three other personnel with AK-47 rifles next to the machine-gun.

SSG Frank and his Afghan platoon began to dismount from the Kamaz truck and to set up a firing support position and a security element next to a main road junction near the compound. SSG Frank and his Afghan platoon set up two M-50-mm mortar guns for indirect fire support if needed.

The rest of the element continued to move slowly toward the compound. SGT Marco—the gunner on my vehicle—chatted over the team radio and said, "Sergeant Zapata, I also have a visual view of the machine-gun target with the M-240 machine-gun aiming sights and am ready to start shooting in case anything happens as we move closer to the compound."

"Continue watching for anything unusual," I responded. "If you see the barrel of the machine-gun pointing our direction, or anyone pointing a weapon at us, you are cleared to fire."

During these few moments, as we drew closer to the compound, I felt as if we were moving in slow motion, expecting an ambush at any moment. Luckily, nothing happened. We were able to reach the main entrance of the compound and several personnel dressed in mixed military and civilian uniforms greeted us.

SFC Kelly and his Afghan assault element occupied the area and set up security inside and outside the compound. The Afghan soldiers stayed visible, walking inside and outside of the compound. SFC Drum and SSG Brink and three PSYOPS personnel moved into a small adobe mud building identified as the medical clinic, located outside the main entrance of the compound.

SFC Wilder and SGT Marco positioned themselves outside, near the main entrance of the compound, with our gun truck. The two Civil Affairs personnel, an interpreter, the Afghan company commander, and I entered the compound. We were escorted into a building with a large room, occupied by several village chiefs and warlord commanders sitting on the floor, waiting for us.

TEA WITH THE WARLORDS

They offered us each a cup of hot Afghan tea to drink during the meeting. Our meeting lasted two hours. We talked about several issues, including providing additional medical supplies and medicine—and providing better patient care for the surrounding villages. We also discussed future construction plans for building water pump storage, medical clinics, and a school in Sarobi. All these plans would need prior approval by the United States Army Civil Affairs and Psychological Operations Command (USACAPOC) in order to be funded.

I asked if the warlord commanders could provide us with any information on Taliban or Al Qaeda activity in the surrounding areas. One of the warlord commanders commented that several of his village people had reported seeing three or four men carrying AK-47 rifles and RPG weapons, with two mules carrying cargo, crossing the Pakistan border into Afghanistan three weeks earlier. Their exact location was unknown.

None of the village chiefs or warlord commanders could give me better or more detailed information on Taliban or Al Qaeda activity near the Pakistan border or near their area.

Our meeting was finished, and we continued to check out their compound for any other large weapons or ammunition caches. We especially checked the serviceability of the Chinese Type-75 anti-aircraft machine gun mounted on the building rooftop. The weapon was found to be in good condition and operational. No ammunition was located for it, however. We questioned the warlords as to how they got the machine-gun. Their response was that they had captured the weapon during the Russian war campaign.

We noticed that the warlord commanders' men were all carrying Russian AK-47 rifles with limited ammunitions for their weapons. We were not able to locate any other kind of weapons, such as RPGs, mortar guns, mines, explosives, large ammunition caches, additional AK-47 rifles, or military radios.

We told the warlord commanders that we would return to the compound at a later time to bring additional medical and medicine supplies. I also said we would be removing the large Chinese Type-75 anti-aircraft machine gun from the compound as soon as possible. We had completed our mission tasking at Sarobi, so we returned to Orgun-e Firebase the same day.

Meeting with village warlord commanders in Sarobi

*Sergeant Zapata completes meeting with village chiefs
and warlords*

MSG Zapata with village warlords and their people

Village warlords—and front view of their compound

Gunner with Chinese Type-75 anti-aircraft machine gun

Afghan Company Commander reviewing Type-75 machine gun

Mujahideen sniper in Sarobi compound

CHAPTER ELEVEN

TALIBAN ATTACK ON ORGUN-E KALAN FIREBASE

Several days had passed, and things were going well with our detachment and our Afghan infantry company. It was early in the morning before sunrise, and the sky was looking gray and cloudy. The temperature was extremely cold but bearable. Looking through the window, I could see snow on the tops of the surrounding mountains.

Each of my team members went to check on their assigned Afghan infantry platoons for the status report accountability of personnel. SFC Kelly and I stayed in the team room, reviewing our order-of-battle situational map on the wall.

We were preparing another mission tasking to complete. Our A-Team and Afghan company were preparing to conduct village patrols and establish checkpoints to gain information on possible terrorist cells located along suspected Taliban and Al Qaeda movement routes.

SFC Kelly and I were trying to analyze on the map possible areas and routes that might be good for selecting and setting up several security checkpoints. A few minutes had passed, when suddenly I heard the unmistakable hiss of a bomb about to go off, then a loud deafening "Boom!" I could hear the sound of one exploding mortar round or rocket hitting outside the firebase perimeter.

131

Everyone began yelling, "Incoming rounds!"

It was a total surprise for us—an unexpected attack. We grabbed our AN/PRC-148 MBITR radios, weapons, and body armor vests and ran outside the building to a nearby fighting position. I was watching everyone scrambling for cover and to their designated bunker positions, when again, I heard the hissing sounds of a bomb about to go off—then a loud "Boom! Boom!"—the sounds of two exploding rockets. One hit inside the firebase near the Tactical Operation Center and one outside, near the main entrance of the firebase.

The 82nd Airborne Division observation points and the Afghan troops had identified the location and direction of the incoming mortar or rocket attacks. SFC Kelly and I turned on our MBITR radios to the internal Advanced Operational Base radio frequency channel to monitor any communication traffic.

I heard the radio operator from observation point number #1. The operator was located in the southwest corner of the firebase, and was giving the location and direction of the enemy attacks. The Airborne infantry soldier on southwest tower number #1 was the Forward Observer (FO) for the mortar gun crews in our firebase. Sergeant Garcia—the FO on the tower—was adjusting and bracketing the fire rounds on the suspected enemy target location.

ATTACK AND COUNTER-ATTACK

I saw several 82nd Airborne personnel by their six mortar guns, yelling and screaming commands at the mortar gun crews. The gun crews fired four to eight high-explosive mortar rounds toward the suspected location of the enemy forces. Within seconds, I saw the impact and heard the echoing sounds of the eight mortar rounds hitting near the suspected enemy locations: "Boom! Boom! Boom!"

I saw the black and white smoke marking the suspected enemy location. As the smoke drifted away, I was able to see the actual location from which the enemy attack had originated. The enemy target was located approximately two miles southeast, on top of a mountain ridge.

Again, I heard another hissing sound of a bomb about to go off—

then the loud "Boom!" I could see the rocket exploding as it hit inside the Afghan National Army tent compound. All I could see now was the black and gray smoke in the air.

Several minutes passed, and I began to communicate with our team members and Afghan company personnel for their status report and accountability. Luckily, we had no damage or injuries among our team members. SFC Kelly and I reported to the Tactical Operations Center to check in with their personnel on any damage or injuries. Fortunately, they too had suffered no injuries or damage.

The firebase commander was busy on the order-of-battle situational map, plotting possible locations of the Taliban. The AOB commander was busy coordinating with the 82nd Airborne infantry company commander and the Quick Reaction Force commanders. The AOB commander and the QRF commanders were coordinating as to the best location to airmobile insert QRF personnel. The plan was to locate and surround the enemy forces on the mountain range.

As I looked around, I saw the other two A-Team commanders and team sergeants coordinating with the firebase commander on plans of action to take. The tentative plan was to airmobile insert the 82nd Airborne troops on the ground to encircle the Taliban, keeping them from escaping and crossing back into Pakistan over the border.

Forty-five minutes later, three Army CH-47 Chinooks were arriving in Orgun-e Firebase to transport the 82nd Airborne QRF Quick Reaction Force. One A-Team from Alpha Company and two Afghan infantry platoons began moving in vehicles near the suspected Taliban location. Once they reached their destination, they began to dismount and move by foot to search and locate the enemy.

Thirty minutes later, one A-Team from Charlie Company was loading a Blackhawk helicopter and departing the firebase to locate and intercept the Taliban movement. I heard the sounds of the rotary blades and the engines starting as one of the Apache Attack helicopters prepared to provide emergency close air support for the ground forces. The Apache would also be assisting in the search for the Taliban.

As for our A-Team and Afghan infantry company, we were to continue on our mission tasking on village patrols. Our team would be setting up security checkpoints and searches near suspected Taliban route movements behind the mountain ranges from which their attacks had come. It was going to be a long day chasing the Taliban in the mountains.

82nd Airborne infantry troops

Army CH-47 Chinooks arriving at Orgun-e Firebase

Transporting infantry troops to interdict the Taliban

82nd Airborne troops loading CH-47s

Departure of 82nd Airborne infantry platoons

Final loading of 82nd Airborne (QRF) on CH-47s

Orgun-e Firebase landing zone and ammunition point

CHAPTER TWELVE

SECURITY CHECKPOINTS AT PIR GOWTI AND DEMYANAY

As the 82nd Airborne and Special Forces units continued their search for the Taliban attackers on Orgun-e Firebase, our A-Team was on the road to execute our village patrols and security checkpoints located at villages named Pir Gowti and Demyanay.

The first village, Pir Gowti, was approximately eleven miles away from Orgun-e Firebase—and from Pir Gowti to Demyanay was another four miles. Both villages were located southeast, directly behind the mountain range where the Taliban had recently executed their initial rocket or mortar attacks on Orgun-e Firebase.

Our A-Team's mission tasking was to execute village patrols and set up checkpoints on main roads and routes leading into and away from the two villages, and if possible, to intercept or capture any of the escaping Taliban forces passing through the villages of Pir Gowti and Demyanay. The villages were four miles apart from each other and another three miles away from the Pakistan border.

Once we arrived at the villages, we stopped and questioned any suspicious persons or village sympathizers to gain information on terrorist cells operating in the villages or along suspected Taliban movement routes. During our security checkpoints, we would be searching every vehicle and questioning all personnel in the vehicles as to where they were going, where they were coming from, and what they were doing. We would be physically searching through their personal belongings. And we would be looking at their hands and faces for signs of powder burns, acid burns, and missing digits. Such injuries were signs of the Taliban working with unstable explosives and ammunitions.

We were also looking for any other types of weapons or explosives, or special demolition equipment tools, that they might be carrying. We knew from past experience that Taliban and Al Qaeda personnel suffered frequent accidents and injuries in working with unstable rockets and explosives as they worked with old rockets and explosives. Lack of experience in working with unstable explosives, rockets, and other ammunitions was an ongoing reality for the enemy.

Our order of movement to the villages Pir Gowti and Demayanay was as follows:

- ▶ Vehicle #1—SFC Wilder, SGT Marco, and I.
- ▶ Vehicle #2—SSG Frank, Afghan interpreter, with thirty Afghan soldiers on a Kamaz transport truck.
- ▶ Vehicle #3—SFC Kelly, Afghan interpreter, with thirty Afghan soldiers on a Kamaz transport truck.
- ▶ Vehicle #4—SFC Drum and SSG Brink.

The plan of execution was to travel to a certain location from which we would move to our designated areas. SFC Kelly and his Afghan platoon executed village patrols and set up two security checkpoints on the north and south ends of Demayanay. SFC Drum and SSG Brink were attached in working with SFC Kelly in working the security checkpoints. SSG Frank and his Afghan platoon were also executing village patrols and set up two security checkpoints in Pir Gowti. SFC Wilder, SGT Marco, and I were attached in working with SSG Frank on working the security checkpoints.

As we reached our release point near the outer city limits of Pir Gowti, SFC Wilder and I and one Afghan squad set up a security checkpoint on a dirt road at the north end of the village. SGT Marco and another Afghan squad set up another security checkpoint on the south end of the village. SSG Frank and two Afghan squads would be executing village foot patrols in the interior of the village. SFC Kelly, SFC Drum, SSG Brink, and one Afghan platoon continued to move to Demayanay to set up their security checkpoints and execute village foot patrols.

After several hours of village patrols, searching inside vehicles, and questioning suspicious persons, I heard on our team radio the communication status report between our Orgun-e Firebase, the 82nd Airborne, and Army Special Forces units. The units were unable to locate any of the Taliban forces on the mountain range. They were still planning to continue their search in a different area.

Hours later, the American Special Forces units notified the Orgun-e Firebase that they had located several modified rocket-launching pad platforms. The rockets that had been fired had left powder burns on the rocks. Also, they found electrical wires on the ground, where the rockets had been fired. The Taliban had built several rocket platforms from which to fire their rockets into Orgun-e Firebase with reasonable accuracy of hitting it.

Several hours had passed, and it was already sunset, when suddenly we heard automatic weapons being fired at a distance, coming from the south end of the village Pir Gowti. I immediately communicated by radio with SSG Frank, who was on foot patrol in the village. I asked him if he had heard any of the shots. He replied that he too had heard the shots south of the village and was moving quickly by foot in that direction. I also communicated with SGT Marco, who was located at the south end of the village in a security checkpoint.

"SGT Marco, what's going on over in your area?" I asked. "I heard sounds of automatic weapons being fired?"

SGT Marco came over the radio to explain what was happening at his security checkpoint.

"Hey, Sergeant Zapata," he replied, "we had a suspicious vehicle with four male subjects approach our security checkpoint. The vehicle continued toward the checkpoint, moving at a high rate of speed, and refused to stop. The Afghan squad yelled several commands to stop, but the vehicle kept moving forward. The Afghan squad fired several rounds from their Russian RPD light machine-gun into the front end of the vehicle. The vehicle then came to an immediate stop several meters from our security checkpoint, and the hajis in the vehicle jumped out of the car with their hands in the air, frightened and yelling not to shoot anymore. Luckily, nobody got injured or killed during the shooting."

As we questioned why they had not stopped, SGT Marco continued, "They were not able to see us or hear our commands as they drove to our position. They were also afraid to stop. We are now searching their vehicle and personal belongings. No illegal items are found as of yet. The hajis will be released to continue to drive away if nothing is found. The vehicle is an old white Toyota car."

I responded back to SGT Marco and said, "SGT Marco, make sure you get all personal information on these guys before you release them."

Minutes later, I heard on the team radio that the 82nd Airborne and Special Forces teams were to return to Orgun-e Firebase. I had communicated with our A-Team to end their mission tasking and return to our rally point as soon as possible. We all linked up at our designated rally point near Pir Gowti and started to drive back to our firebase.

It had been a long day searching for the Taliban, and we'd had no luck finding their locations. We had collected little information of any value to use for tracking Taliban or Al Qaeda activities. All collected information from the villagers was unreliable information—inaccurate locations and times of possible sightings of Taliban movements in the surrounding villages. We continued to check these areas, regardless of the information given to us.

Once in Orgun-e Firebase, we debriefed the AOB commander on the results of our mission tasking, and later on we turned in an after-action report on the mission tasking we had just completed. We now turned our attention to planning for the next mission tasking.

Security Checkpoints at Pir Gowti and Demyanay

Team assembly area

Arrival in the village Pir Gowti

SSG Frank returning from village patrol

CHAPTER THIRTEEN

ATTACK ON VILLAGE QARYA-I-SAYKH

Throughout the most recent several days, SFC Kelly and I had interrogated several surrounding villagers and village chiefs and offered cash rewards for reliable information on Taliban or Al Qaeda activities in our surrounding area.

The U.S. Army was offering bounty reward money of up to $5,000 or more, depending on credibility and importance of the information—and a guarantee of the identity and location of Taliban or Al Qaeda personnel. We soon received reliable information from a disgruntled village chief who was willing to give us detailed information on a large Taliban cache site near a village called Qarya-I-Saykh.

This village was located southwest and ten miles away from Orgun-e Firebase. In addition to the cache site, a safe house used by the Taliban terrorist cells was located nearby. The size of the enemy force located in these sites would range from four to ten heavily armed personnel.

Our mission tasking would be a joint operation with another A-Team from one of the other companies—and two Afghan infantry companies. The mission would require separate raids on two large adobe mud-structure compounds located close together in the village of Qarya-I-Saykh. Both compounds were surrounded by high adobe mud walls, protecting an interior courtyard with watchtowers

145

at each corner of the compound. Our mission was to search and destroy Taliban cache sites and collect intelligence data.

As both A-Teams and Afghan companies prepared for the operation, the informant was detained safely inside the firebase and was not allowed to depart. The informant would be used in leading us to the suspected Taliban site, and the capture of terrorists and equipment at the cache site would need to be guaranteed prior to receiving his reward money.

We gave an operations order plan to all the troops and the AOB commander in the morning. The order of movement to the targets was first, one A-Team from Alpha Company, with one Afghan company and their two interpreters. Next in the order of movement would be our own A-Team from Charlie Company, with one Afghan company and our two interpreters. The transportation for both A-Teams and Afghan troops would be by vehicles to our designated objective rally point. The organizational structure for both A-Teams and the Afghan companies, once at their targets, was to organize into three separate elements—assault, support, and security.

As we drove closer to our targets, we stopped, dismounted our vehicles, and then moved into a tentative objective rally point to plan and reorganize and to send out a leaders' recon with the informant to confirm the two target locations. The leaders' recon element from both A-Teams consisted of MSG Zapata, SSG Brink, SGT Marco, MSG Douglas, SSG Ashley, SFC Levin and the informant. Once we completed the leaders' recon and confirmed both targets, we left SGT Marco and SFC Ashley as the surveillance team to observe both targets. The rest of the leaders' recon element returned to our position and disseminated updated information about the targets to the element leaders from both A-Teams and the Afghan soldiers.

Action at the target was that both A-Teams continued to occupy their positions. Then, our own A-Team reached our designated target. Our A-Team security element was composed of SFC Drum and SSG Brink—and one Afghan platoon. Our security element providing protection to the left, right, and rear of our assault and support elements.

Our support element was composed of SSG Frank, SGT Marco,

and one Afghan platoon. They were located approximately four hundred meters to our left flank inside a wide, deep, dry creek bed, from which they observed the compound.

Our assault element was made up of SFC Kelly, SFC Wilder, and I, plus two Afghan platoons with one interpreter. Our assault element was now in position three hundred meters away in a prone position, inside a wide three-foot-deep orchard irrigation trench near the compound.

As we waited with both Afghan platoons inside this irrigation trench, we observed one person with an AK-47 rifle and a second person with an RPG-7 rocket-propelled grenade launcher on top of the northwest tower—and a third person with an AK-47 rifle located in front of the main entrance gate of the compound.

The plan was for both A-Teams and their Afghan companies to get into position and execute the attacks on both targets simultaneously. Several minutes had passed, when the second A-Team radio operator from Alpha Company spoke over my MBITR radio, giving me the signal that they were in position and ready to attack the Taliban safe house target. As I acknowledged the call, I gave the signal that our A-Team personnel were also ready to execute the attack on the cache site in the compound.

"Tango"—The Attack Commences

Seconds later, I heard my MBITR radio squelch sound come over the radio—then I heard the code word "tango" coming from the second A-Team radio operator—the signal for the assault elements to execute the attacks on both targets. I signaled SFC Kelly and SFC Wilder for our assault element to start moving quickly toward the compound. At the same time, I began to hear at a distance the whopping sounds of helicopter blades approaching fast.

I grabbed my AN/PRC-117 radio to monitor aviation traffic. I heard the pilots in two Apache attack helicopters trying to communicate with both our A-Teams to provide emergency close air support (ECAS) as we attacked the targets. The Apache helicopters were identified as Rhino-one-zero and Rhino-two-zero. I acknowledged the call from both pilots, identifying myself as Falcon-niner-five.

"Rhino-one-zero, Rhino-two-zero, this is Falcon-niner-five, over."

"Falcon-niner-five, this is Rhino-two-zero assigned to you as your close air support, over."

"Rhino-two-zero, this is Falcon-niner-five, roger. Do a sweep over the target and identify any threats, over."

"Falcon-niner-five, this is Rhino-two-zero, roger."

The Apache attack helicopter began flying in a figure-eight pattern, looking like a vulture hunting for its prey. The pilot began to communicate and said he had spotted two personnel on top of the building carrying an AK-47 rifle and an RPG—and one armed person at the main entrance of the compound. He also was able to observe other personnel but unable to identify if they were a threat or carrying weapons.

Suddenly, I heard shots being fired, coming from Alpha Company A-Team's location. I suspected now that the other A-Team was under fire from the enemy. As we continued to move faster toward our own target, trying to reach the main entrance of the compound, the Rhino-two-zero Apache attack helicopter began circling over the enemy targets on our compound. I could see Rhino-two-zero's area weapons system aiming and rotating its M230 chain gun, capable of firing 30-mm rounds at 625 rounds per minute on the spotted enemy targets. Any threatening move from the suspected enemy, and the Apache helicopter would have fired its weapons on personnel, tearing them to pieces. The suspected Taliban were lucky the Apache helicopter had not fired on them. Rhino-two-zero began to egress east away from the target, calling me over the radio.

"Falcon-niner-five, this is Rhino-two-zero, over."

"Rhino-two-zero, this is Falcon-niner-five, go ahead, over."

"Falcon-niner-five, this is Rhino-two-zero. Unable to see additional targets. Cleared to enter compound, over."

"Rhino-two-zero, this is Falcon-niner-five, roger. Out."

As the Apache attack helicopter moved away from the target, we began moving quickly toward the compound. As we reached the main entrance gate, I had one Afghan platoon begin to establish a 360-degree security perimeter around the outside walls of the compound. Simultaneously, SFC Kelly, SFC Wilder, and their Afghan platoon entered the compound and began to clear rooms and secure the area inside.

I heard several shots being fired as they and the Afghan platoon entered the main entrance gate. As I too entered through the main gate into the courtyard, I could see Afghan forces detaining one Taliban suspect on the ground, who had been seen carrying one AK-47 rifle near the gate entrance.

ANA Forces and SFC Wilder quickly rushed across the courtyard, entering rooms to search and clear them of any other suspects or threats. Minutes had passed, when SFC Kelly called me on the internal team radio to meet him on top of the northwest tower.

"Sergeant Zapata, you need to come and look at this shit."

INTERROGATING TALIBAN SUSPECTS

As I continued to move toward SFC Kelly's location, I saw SFC Wilder and his ANA squad carefully looking at a large pile of mortar rounds near one of the rooms inside the courtyard. I was able to reach the northwest tower, where SFC Kelly and the Afghan company commander were located. As I approached them, I saw that they had two Taliban suspects who had been seen carrying AK-47 rifles. The suspects were being interrogated by SFC Kelly and the Afghan commander. On the ground next to them was a rocket-propelled grenade launcher (RPG) with several RPG rounds—and two AK-47 rifles.

We continued to search and clear the area for more Taliban, weapons, and munitions. SFC Wilder was busy and had discovered over 200 Russian 82-mm mortar rounds and over fifty RPGs located inside one of the rooms they had searched. As we inspected the mortar rounds, we noticed that all of them were loaded and prepared to fire, with the primer shells already inserted. The primers were the size of a 12-gauge shotgun shell. The Russian 82-mm mortar rounds looked gray-blue in color, rusty and dirty, yet usable to fire.

We loaded all the live mortar rounds and RPG rounds onto the Russian Kamaz transport truck. We had completed our mission tasking on our target, and things were looking good. It was amazing that no one had gotten hurt during this mission. Several minutes had passed, when Alpha Company's second A-Team radio operator called me on my MBITER radio. They needed additional help clearing and searching their second compound for hidden cache sites buried in an orchard field. Their compound was located seven hundred meters from our compound.

SFC Kelly, SFC Wilder, two Afghan squads, and I started to walk toward the second target. As we entered the compound into the courtyard, we could see two suspects being questioned and detained by American and Afghan Forces. We saw in the far corner of the courtyard a small orchard field, with several dug-out trenches and several Afghan soldiers digging in the trenches. Inside the trenches were located hundreds of RPG rounds; 64-mm rockets; 70-mm rockets; small arms munitions; explosives; American, Russian, and French radio equipment; RPG launchers; and RPK machine-guns.

All these items were recovered and loaded onto a Russian Kamaz transport truck to take back to Orgun-e Firebase for disposal. Again, luckily, no one from both A-Teams or from among the Afghan soldiers had been hurt during the attacks on both compounds.

As SFC Kelly and I continued to look around the outside of the compound, we noticed several adobe mud homes near the compound. Then suddenly, we saw children coming outside of their mud homes to watch us. I waved at them to come to our location in order to talk to them, but the children were frightened and kept away in fear of what was going on around them. Afterward, they started to move slowly toward us, and we gave them Meals-Ready-to-Eat candy. Before we knew it, we were talking and taking photos of the children. I wondered what these children were thinking or going through during all the yelling and shouting that had happened during our initial attack on both compounds.

Several hours had passed, and we had completed our mission tasking on both targets. All weapons, munitions, explosives, and items of radio equipment were loaded on the Kamaz vehicles. All Taliban suspects were interrogated and later released to a U.S. Military Police unit for additional questioning.

We immediately began to return to Orgun-e Firebase to debrief our mission to the AOB commander and write an after-action report on the operation. As I drove back on one of the Russian Kamaz trucks loaded with possibly unstable primers inside the mortar rounds and rockets, I realized how crazy it was of me riding back there, with the possibility of these ammunitions of exploding.

But luckily, nobody got hurt during this mission tasking, and I would live another day to tell another story—as the missions and days began to get even more dangerous.

John inspecting mortar rounds

Sergeant Zapata inspecting mortar rounds

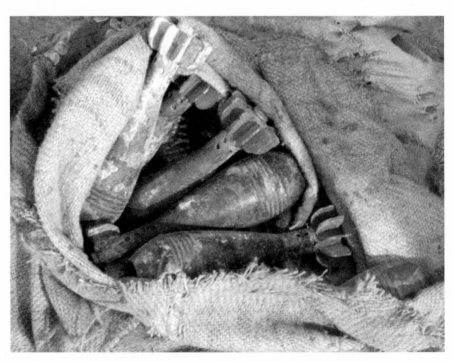

82-mm mortar rounds with fuse inside bag

Afghan soldiers counting mortar rounds

Afghan soldiers loading mortar rounds on rear of truck

Sergeant Zapata and Jim inspecting captured RPG rounds

Jim getting ready to destroy RPG rounds and unstable explosives

*Sergeant Zapata inside trench with hidden RPG rounds,
64-mm rockets, and 70-mm rockets*

64-mm rockets and RPG rounds

Captured American, Russian, and French military radios

Captured DPM machine guns and radios

Sergeant Zapata and John with Afghan village children

Afghan village children pose for a photo

Translator and Sergeant Zapata with village children

Afghan company commander

Afghan commander and his platoon

Sergeant Zapata's translator Ahmad

MSG Zapata after the village attack

CHAPTER FOURTEEN

CACHE SITE AT VILLAGE TANI

On January 25, 2003, we were preparing for our last joint mission tasking on a village called Tani, located in the Khowst Province. The village of Tani was located forty-four miles northeast of Orgun-e Firebase. Our mission was to search and destroy a large cache site of weapons, ammunitions, explosives, and any enemy personnel.

Together, both U.S. Special Forces A-Teams from AOB Orgun-e had spent several weeks of hard work collecting information from the surrounding villagers and tribal chiefs and offering reward money for information leading to the capture of any Taliban or Al Qaeda personnel or location of their activities. One late afternoon, we were once again able to receive reliable information of several personnel protecting a large cache site armed with two air defense artillery guns on the target.

Early the next morning, both U.S. Army Special Forces A-Teams and one Afghan infantry company were issued an operations order for the plan of attack on the cache site located in the village Tani. The order of movement to the target was first, one A-Team from Alpha Company and two Afghan platoons—and their two Afghan translators. The second order of movement would be our own A-Team from Charlie Company with our two translators and one Afghan platoon. The transportation, for both A-Teams and Afghan troops, would be by vehicles to our designated tentative objective rally point.

As before, the organizational structure for both A-Teams and the Afghan company, once at the target, was to organize into three separate elements—assault, support, and security. We also had two Apache attack helicopters escorting and providing emergency close air support during our movement to the target and once at the target area.

We departed Orgun-e Firebase in the morning in order to reach our target before nightfall. Our journey to the target would take us several hours, passing through rugged mountains, dangerous and deep canyons, and hostile territory. We had driven for two hours and we were now entering an open valley, able to see the village of Tani.

As we approached the village, I could see the two Apache helicopters flying over our vehicles toward the village. I heard the pilots trying to communicate with both of our A-Teams to provide emergency close air support as we approached our targets.

For this mission, the Apache helicopters were identified as Blazer-one-zero and Blazer-two-zero. I grabbed my AN/PRC-117 radio to monitor aviation radio traffic. I acknowledged the call from both pilots and identified myself as Zulu-niner-five.

"Blazer-one-zero, Blazer-two-zero, this is Zulu-niner-five, over."

"Zulu-niner-five, this is Blazer-two-zero. We are making a sweep over the target to identify threat targets, over."

"Blazer-two-zero, this is Zulu-niner-five, roger."

HUNTING FOR PREY

I watched the Apache helicopters flying in a figure-eight pattern, looking again like vultures hunting for prey to kill. One pilot began to communicate and said he had spotted two unoccupied air defense artillery guns. They were Chinese Type-75 anti-aircraft machine guns capable of firing 14.5-caliber rounds. One Type-75 machine gun was located northeast of the village, on top of a religious Mosque. The second Type-75 machine gun was on the ground near a second building, located at the southwest entrance of Tani. Both weapons had 360 degrees of clear visibility for their fields of fire on any target approaching the village.

The pilot was able to identify several armed personnel in uniforms with AK-47 rifles, near an ammunition supply point at the main entrance of the village. The pilot could see other personnel but was unable to tell whether they were carrying weapons.

We began to deploy to our designated positions to begin the attack on Tani. Our A-Team and one Afghan platoon were responsible for providing the security and blocking positions surrounding the village of Tani. Our A-Teams' mission was to stop Taliban or Al Qaeda personnel from escaping or entering the village of Tani while the attack was taking place. The second A-Team from Alpha Company and two Afghan platoons immediately occupied their assault and support positions and concurrently continued their entrance into the village to locate the cache site.

During the attack on the village, we had captured and located two large cache sites with unstable explosives, munitions, and large weapon systems. SFC Wilder, SGT Marco, and SSG Frank provided additional help in identifying, labeling, and destroying the unstable explosives, munitions, and weapon systems found inside the cache sites.

We were unable to locate or capture any Taliban or Al Qaeda suspects in the village of Tani. Luckily, we had no injuries during this operation. It was amazing that not a single shot had been fired during the operation. We had captured numerous munitions and loaded them onto Russian Kamaz trucks to transport back to the AOB. The mission was completed, and we began our return to Orgun-e Firebase. Our drive back to Orgun-e was a long, tiresome journey. We arrived back at 1 a.m. and unloaded some of the captured ammunition and equipment. Later on, I turned in our team's after-action report on the mission. By the time we all got to sleep, it was 3:30 a.m.

The next two days at Orgun-e Firebase were spent packing and loading all our A-Team's equipment. Our new orders were to return to Kabul Military Training Center for additional mission tasking. Our transportation to Kabul was going to be on a convoy of three Russian Kamaz transport trucks. The journey by land to Kabul took us fourteen hours. We were lucky, because we had traveled through some dangerous enemy territory without getting ambushed. The weather that day was cold, overcast, rainy—just plain bad. The terrain was covered with snow, muddy, wet, rugged, and isolated from any outside help. We were traveling off road and cross country, driving three Russian Kamaz transport trucks with two Toyota pickup gun-trucks as security force escorts. Our travel route selection forced us not to use or see any roads for several hours. I was surprised that the vehicles were able to travel in that type of terrain and under those weather conditions.

We finally reached Kabul Military Training Center safely late in the evening after 10 p.m. We immediately reported to the FOB Operations Center for a debriefing.

Later that night we began to unload some of our sensitive equipment from the Kamaz transport trucks. By that time we were tired and ready to catch some sleep and awaited for further instuctions from our company commander the next morning for further mission taskings.

That night we were happy to have lived to see another day and tell another story.

Inspecting unstable explosives and munitions

Variety of Russian mortar rounds and bullets

Inspecting more munitions

Type-75 anti-aircraft machine gun ammunitions

Sergeant Zapata and Afghan officer with Chinese Type-75 machine gun

Mosque with Type-75 anti-aircraft machine gun on rooftop

Afghan Mosque with Type-75 anti-aircraft machine gun

SSG Frank on Toyota gun truck, resting before moving out again

Destroying unstable explosives and munitions

The end result of a destroyed cache site

Final team photo

Another final photo of the team

CHAPTER FIFTEEN

NEW AFGHAN FIREBASE IN GARDEZ

It was early in March, and we had returned from our last mission in Orgun-e Kalan. We began to hear rumors that American military forces were getting ready to invade Iraq, and yet other rumors that we were getting ready to return back home.

In March 2003, our operational detachment commander had finally arrived at the Kabul Military Training Center. We were glad to have Captain Cole join our A-Team once again. We all noticed that Captain Cole was eager to do something with our team before our entire battalion returned home. I felt the burden had lifted from my shoulders when Captain Cole took over as the commander. I no longer had to attend the officer staff meetings at battalion.

We were also glad to have another new team member assigned to ODA995. His name was SSG Little, and he would be working as the junior Special Forces medical sergeant on the team. SSG Little was a tall, physically fit individual with dark hair, and he was excited about being on the team and eager about going on a mission soon.

The morale of our A-Team was good, but we were tired and ready to return home. By this time all, our team members were eager to leave Afghanistan and move on to bigger and better things in life. We had all seen what war was like in Afghanistan. On March 1, 2003, the FOB was tasking our ODA995 with one last mission—to build a new Afghan firebase near Gardez in Pakita Province, Afghanistan. The location of the new firebase was seventy miles southwest of Kabul, near the town called Gardez.

Our A-Team had put together a plan of action on how we were going to build and provide logistical support for this new Afghan Gardez firebase. The firebase had to be of a size to provide accommodations for three Afghan infantry companies. Within two days our A-Team gave the FOB commander a mission briefing on the execution of building a new Afghan firebase near Gardez. ODA995 had received approval from the FOB commander on the plan of action, so we immediately began to execute the operation.

The plan was to use a split-team concept and take two Afghan platoons for this operation. Our detachment would be operating as an A-Team and a B-Team for this mission. Several team members would stay back at the KMTC as a logistical support element for our detachment, while half of the other team continued to build the firebase.

Personnel going forward to build the Afghan firebase included Capt. Cole, SFC Kelly, SFC Drum, SSG Frank, SSG Brink, SSG Little, and SFC Wilder. SGT Marco and I stayed behind at the FOB, working as logistical support B-Team and as the communications center for the A-Team building the Afghan firebase. ODA995 was required to send daily situational status reports on their activities at the new Afghan Gardez firebase. Our mission back at the FOB was to support our A-Team with any logistical equipment or supplies they requested.

Within days, they were requesting lumber, sandbags, food, water, ammunitions, heavy equipment, and power generators for electricity. In addition to this duty, I had to give the FOB commander a daily briefing on the status of ODA995s activity and on conditions in Gardez.

Two weeks had passed, and ODA995 had built the surrounding security walls for the Gardez firebase. The Team was now requesting additional supplies—they needed more firewood, lumber, food, water, ammunition, and power generators. SGT Marco and myself, with two other support personnel from the battalion, ground transported the supplies to the new Afghan Gardez firebase. We used three Russian Kamaz transport trucks to deliver the requested supplies—and we had two Security Force vehicles to help escort our convoy to the new firebase.

A GYPSY CARAVAN

As we started to drive one morning on our journey to deliver supplies to the Afghan Gardez firebase, I was astonished to see the surrounding terrain—jagged mountains covered with snow—and many local people. Along our route, we encountered a large Afghan Gypsy tribe caravan of many families walking along the roadside.

I was amazed to see how strong these people were from all their traveling from faraway places. The tribe caravan had just crossed the high mountains of Pakistan. The nomadic women were searching and gathering firewood as they walked with their tribe, accompanied by camels, goats, and donkeys. The small children rode on camels as they traveled. The camels and donkeys carried all their supplies and food to their next destination.

Minutes later, we saw the new Afghan Gardez firebase from a distance. As we approached, I saw the rest of the team members with big smiles on their faces. I met with Captain Cole and the other team members. We started to unload the equipment and supplies from the Russian Kamaz transport trucks.

Afterward, we all chatted about how the work of building the firebase was going and about the rumors of war with Iraq—and of when we might possibly be returning home. By mid afternoon, I departed the Afghan Gardez Firebase and drove the Russian Kamaz transport truck back to KMTC Firebase. The trip took us two hours. Again, we were lucky to make it back to KMTC safely before dark without any problems or injuries.

Several days passed, and we started to see the 3rd Special Forces Group advanced party personnel arriving at KMTC. They were getting ready to relieve and rotate our battalion from command. By the end of March, our A-Team returned to KMTC.

DESPERATE LANDS

The new Afghan Gardez Firebase was never totally completed. Our battalion commander told us we were leaving Afghanistan by the first week of April. Our mission was complete in Afghanistan— and we were coming home.

Main entrance gate to Gardez Firebase

Southwest view of firebase

South view of firebase

Afghan soldiers clean dishes in Gardez Firebase

Camels and donkeys help carry their supplies

Gypsy nomadic tribe crossing the Pakistan border

Camels carrying food and supplies

Camels carrying heavy loads for tribe families

Gypsy nomadic tribe with entire family

Afghan nomadic women and children walking in native dress

Afghan gypsy nomadic women carrying firewood

Gyspy nomaic women searching for firewood

A look of hope from an Afghan child

Camels—one carrying an Afghan child

An Afghan child bundled into a jacket

Baby camels aboard adult camels

Camels carry tent poles for a shelter

Camels and donkeys carrying food, wood, and supplies

Gypsy nomadic children walking

Gypsy tribe crossing the Pakistan border

Camels and tribesmen crossing the Pakistan border

CHAPTER SIXTEEN

WELCOME HOME-COMING

By April 15, 2003, we were packing all our team equipment into our steel A-Team storage containers. We were excited to be leaving Afghanistan. Prior to departure, the battalion operations center prepared a flight manifest list with the names of soldiers leaving Afghanistan. This flight manifest would show which personnel were going on each aircraft and the arrival times back at Fort Carson, Colorado.

The entire 5th Battalion, 19th Special Forces Group was scheduled to fly back to Fort Carson in separate groups and on different dates and at different times. Not all of the soldiers would be coming home at once but rather in "waves" of small units.

An Air Force C-17 aircraft would pick us up at the Kabul Airport by mid morning. Transportation would be by bus to the Kabul Airport, and we had two Security Force vehicles from the 82nd Airborne escorting our convoy to the airport.

Minutes later the C-17 aircraft landed, and it was an incredible sight to watch this huge aircraft taxi into our area. The rear ramp began to open, and several Air Force crew chief personnel waved at us to start loading our equipment onto the aircraft. The Air Force crew began to load our large pallets and equipment containers into the aircraft first. Within an hour, we were loaded onto the aircraft and leaving Kabul, Afghanistan, for the last time.

I will always remember two days prior to our departure from Afghanistan, when our battalion commander gave us a safety briefing before we left the Kabul Military Training Center Firebase. The Commander said,

"Because of security reasons and a possible terrorist attack threat on our aircraft landing at Peterson Air Force base in Colorado," the commander said, "we will not be having a 'Welcome Home-Coming' committee reception when we arrive in Colorado."

He continued by telling us that he did not want any of our family members to be waiting for us at the Peterson Air Force base terminal when we arrived. He made this clear to all personnel, saying, "If I catch or see any soldier's family members waiting at the Peterson Air Force base when we arrive, I will issue an Article Fifteen to the soldier for disobeying my orders."

Dumfounded and Disappointed

Wow! We all stood there dumfounded, looking at the commander and wondered what had happened. It did not make any sense—it sounded crazy. After watching many times on CNN as other welcome-home receptions took place for military units returning from the war in Afghanistan, it was confusing to us as to why we would not be allowed this on our return.

Sometimes, I wondered about the decision-making processes of our leaders in the military and in the civilian political bureaucracy. We had survived the war in Afghanistan and lived to tell the stories to our friends and families. I had served fourteen months during "Operation Enduring Freedom." Other soldiers had served seven months, and we were all lucky to have returned home alive and safe.

We arrived at 8 a.m. at Peterson Air Force Base in Colorado. Several military buses were ready to transport us to Fort Carson. Our reception at the airport terminal was composed of just two civilian airport terminal employees. Their job was to supervise the unloading of our equipment from the aircraft onto military transport trucks. Once our equipment was loaded onto the trucks, we quickly loaded the buses and began our trip back to Fort Carson.

Our entire battalion was required to stay one month at Fort Carson to demobilize all personnel from active duty. During those four weeks, we went through individual medical examinations and out-process procedures for all the soldiers in the battalion. Also during this period, many soldiers had medical evaluation appointments and received medical treatments for injuries received while in Afghanistan.

The entire battalion continued to conduct maintenance and inventory repairs of all our equipment. I was once again assigned to my original company. After being in Fort Carson for one month, our company was released to drive our military vans back to the California Army National Guard Amory. Once our Company arrived at the California Army National Guard Armory, we continued to unload equipment and to perform equipment repairs and take inventory.

Several days later, the California Army National Guard command decided to have a quick media press release of our arrival and wanted to have a small award ceremony for our soldiers. Not too many people or supporters showed up that morning at the National Guard Armory for the award ceremony. I guess it was a lack of coordination and planning on someone's part. It was a quick ceremony, and not too many people stayed around afterward, as I remember. Even our California Army National Guard Office of the Adjutant General (OTAG) command did not stay long to mingle with the soldiers and enjoy soft drinks and eat food.

By June 23, 2003, all military active duty orders were terminated for our unit. All soldiers—including myself—were released to return home and to return to work in their civilian jobs as if nothing had ever happened.

To this day I will always remember how, after completely being separated and retired from the U.S. Department of the Army for two weeks, a U.S. Department of Defense background investigations agent came to my house on a Saturday early morning. The agent identified himself as Agent Clair from DOD and said he was doing an updated (TS) Top Secret security clearance background investigation on me.

I immediately told Agent Clair that I had retired from the U.S.Army Special Forces on 23 June 2003. I also gave him a copy of my retirement military orders. Agent Clair still insisted on doing his investigation and on asking me several personal questions. The agent continued his interview and questioning for an hour and a half before leaving my home.

I was surprised to see a Department of Defense investigator doing a Top Secret background investigation on me, having just returned from Afghanistan and retired from the U.S.Army. The agent's comments were to the effect that I could be called back to active duty even if I had retired.

A few soldiers from the company decided to stay with the California Army National Guard Special Forces. Others decided to go back to full-time active duty in the U.S. Army Special Forces. Still others who were discontented with what they saw got the hell out from their units or retired. All operational detachments had a large turnover of soldiers. The retention of good leadership and experienced noncommissioned officers was at a low point in the unit because of the hardship of long overseas tours and the far better civilian career opportunities or advantages of retirement.

Within a few months, our company had a complete change of leadership command. The company had a new commander and a new sergeant major for the unit. Six months later, I received a call from my old operational detachment Alpha 995 members. SFC Kelly and SFC Wilder told me they were still working with the Colorado Army National Guard Special Forces Group. SSG Frank and SSG Brink went back to active duty, assigned to the 3rd Special Forces Group. SFC Drum and SGT Marco also went back to active duty, assigned to the 5th Special Forces Group.

I often wonder what they are doing now! In conclusion, I never thought in my wildest dreams that I would be taking part in such a large global war on terrorism. The events that took place in Africa and in Afghanistan were all a bad dream to many soldiers. No matter how we all feel about the war situation now or the failures of certain leaders, our soldiers deserve our support and respect. They did the best they were able to do in order to accomplish their missions with the knowledge and support of the American people.

War never goes the way you plan for it to happen. These are some of my memories of the war in Afghanistan, for many of us who were there.

82nd Airborne Security Force protection

Our unit equipment on pallets being loaded aboard aircraft

C-17 aircraft rear door ramp opens for loading

Loading aircraft now!

*First arrival and stop at Uzkekistan Airport —MSG Zapata with
Uzbekistan soldiers*